My Miraculous

Journey with God

with Only $60

and a Suitcase

INGRID APOLLON

WORKBOOK PRESS LLC
187 E Warm Springs Rd,
Suite B285, Las Vegas, NV 89119, USA

Website: https://workbookpress.com/
Hotline: 1-888-818-4856
Email: admin@workbookpress.com

Ordering Information:
Quantity sales. Special discounts are available on quantity purchases by corporations, associations, and others.
For details, contact the publisher at the address above.

Library of Congress Control Number:

ISBN-13:   978-1-958176-96-2 (Paperback Version)

REV. DATE: 22/04/2022

MY MIRACULOUS JOURNEY WITH GOD WITH ONLY $60 AND A SUITCASE

CHAPTER 1

THE EARLY YEARS

Kindergarten and my earliest memories of childhood

It was 1975 and I was five years old. I lived in the projects in New York. When I started school in Kindergarten, I had a peeing problem. I don't remember all in detail but, I remembered I had a teacher named Ms. Gee. All the students would laugh every time we say her name because it reminded us of what someone would say if they wanted to think about something.

"Gee!" I wonder what would happen if I threw a ball at your face!"

"Would your nose swell up?"

We would laugh and make up the sentences and joke around using the word "Gee." We had a lot of fun in class joking around. We would be active all the time in class and try not to have a dull moment. Kindergarten was cool because we would have playtime and go outside. Each table in the classroom had different colors and I sat at the yellow table. It was fun! I loved yellow because it reminded me of the sunshine. I always like to laugh and be happy. I didn't remember if I had a best friend, but I always followed what the other kids were doing. We even had bathrooms near the classroom. I used to pee on myself when I would sit in class. I couldn't get myself to ask to go to the bathroom. I don't know why. If we wanted to go to the bathroom, we had to raise our hands and ask. I just couldn't do it. I couldn't figure out what the issue was. It was embarrassing because the smell would make the classroom stink! I wasn't sure if there was anything wrong, but I guess I couldn't hold it. I know the teacher spoke to my parents about it. My Dad was not around much but my mom probably spoke to her about it. I was always the oddball. It took me time to learn to ask and to speak up! I don't know why I couldn't speak up, but I think I was afraid of what the other kids would say, or maybe I was afraid to admit it. The teacher would always put a paper on my seat for me to sit down on. It was a little embarrassing. I had a lot of fun in a kindergarten class because we played a lot but when I turned six things started to change a little.

Now it's 1976 and I was six years old. Every summer that I can remember, I spent my days in the park playing with my friends. I lived in the projects in New York. I remember the building because ours was the only one that had an American flag in front of it. My father worked for General Motors in New Jersey while my mother stayed at home. I loved my mother and my father, but my brother and I were not always disciplined. We were how can I say- not easy to manage. I remember I would watch how my father treated my mom and we would just follow his behavior. My father used to beat my mother. We would talk back to our mother because we saw our dad did it, and we thought it was okay. We wouldn't dare talk back to my father, though. He was not one to mess with. I was a little scared of him. My brother is two years older than I am. He loved to watch baseball because of my dad. My dad was a true Mets fan! They used to watch the ball game together while I was in my room playing with my dolls. My favorite doll back then was Barbie. My brother also has a good memory.

As a kid, I used to think that he was not human. His brain was like a computer. He would get an A in every class. I thought he was perfect until I saw how the other kids acted towards him. They would tease and make fun of him because of his speech. Sometimes, he was super active, and the kids mocked him for this as well. My brother attended a special school. When he was a child, he couldn't speak until he attended speech classes. As for me, I had a lazy eye. I'm laughing about it now, but I hated wearing glasses back then. I felt wearing glasses was not cool. My father used to force me to wear them. He wore glasses also. I got teased a lot for wearing glasses, but my brother was teased because he was "special." When I mean special, I meant that he was different than the other kids. He was sent to a special school for disabled children when he was young but as he has gotten older, he was a whiz kid. He has a brain like a computer where he has no problem remembering data or facts! He's amazing!

I remember living in the projects. I hated passing by some of the kids because they were not nice. One time, when we took the elevator to our floor, the kids rushed us as the doors opened and pushed my brother around. I was six years old still currently and keep in mind he was two years older than me. I yelled, "Leave him alone!" The kids laughed at me because I was short. They were taller and most of them were older. They knew I couldn't do anything and one of the kids held me back. My brother was helpless. I wanted to beat them up, but I couldn't do anything. All I could do was keep yelling, "Leave him alone! Leave him alone! I always felt like I was his protector, even though he was two years older than me. They pushed us both out of the elevator. I was angry. I used to wish that I were taller and stronger so these things could not happen to us.

One time, I got home from school, and I couldn't find my brother. I asked my mom, and she said he hadn't come home yet. We both began to worry because it was already evening. I told my mom that I was going to look for him. I was wondering why my mother didn't think about looking for him earlier. She probably thought he was coming home with me or maybe he was getting home late from school. Sometimes, he would come home late but not this late when it is near bedtime. I didn't understand why she didn't make the attempt to look for him I know you're probably wondering, why would a parent let a six-year-old child go out at night alone to look for someone? My mother allowed us to go to the park alone since the park was next to our building, so it wasn't far. She would let us go to the store by ourselves at this age. When I look back now, I realized that she should have been more aware of us going out on our own at a young age. As I look back now, I also realized she was not mentally stable. I didn't think about it at the time, but I went to the park and saw some kids, but I didn't see all the bullies. I went to all the parks around our neighborhood and couldn't find him. It was getting pitch dark, so I headed home. On my way back, I sat on a bench and just cried. I kept saying to myself, "Where is he?" It felt like I sat at the bench for fifteen minutes. I then decided to go home since the park was right outside our building. As I got to the apartment, I opened the door and yelled, "Mom!" "Did he get back?" She said, "No."

My Mom called the police and they said, "They'll look for him, but he must be missing at least twenty-four hours. I ran to my room and slammed the door. I went to my bed and closed my eyes, trying not to have any bad thoughts. Within an hour, the doorbell rang. My mother opened the door, and I ran into it. A police officer was standing in the doorway.

He was standing there with my brother and asked, "Ma'am, is this your son?"

She frantically said, "Yes!"

The police said, "Ma'am, your son was up on the roof of the building with some other kids. The kids were bullying him. Luckily, they didn't push him off the roof!"

Listening to him, I was so angry!

My mom said to the officer as he allowed my brother into the apartment, "Thank you for saving my son!" My brother walked in calmly and I asked him, "Are you okay?" He said, "Yes." But he didn't want to talk about it much, so we left him alone to go to his room. He was probably too upset to talk but I don't blame him for an eight-year-old. I was so upset that I went to my room and started getting violent with my dolls. I felt helpless and hopeless because I couldn't help him. I kept taking the doll and banging it on the floor. I probably took the doll's head off and destroyed its body. I wanted to hurt those kids!

After that incident, we didn't see the bullies for a while. I guess the cops must've threatened them. I used to wish that I was confident and courageous like my Dad but my brother feared him also. I used to think my mom loved my brother more than me because she paid more attention to him, but I didn't think at the time it had anything to do with his inability to adapt to certain things. My Dad always paid attention to me. I loved my dad but, at the same time, I was always nervous because of how he treated my mom.

My father was cool and suave. He was the type of guy who, when he walked into a room, everyone would jump up and greet. He was the life of the party! People all saw that charming side of him, but not the violent side. One day, I saw how he treated my mom. It was still when I was six years old that I witnessed this. My dad would come home anytime he want to but, there were even times he would sleep out. When he eventually came home, he would greet my brother and me. I would always jump up and yell, "Daddy!" I was always excited to see my Dad because he would take me to fun places.

I remembered one time he came home and said, "Let's go to the amusement park." I was about eight years old then. He often took me out but not my brother. I also noticed he didn't take my mom out much. On the way to the amusement park, we picked up a lady. I noticed that the lady and my dad were holding hands and he hugged and kissed her.

I privately asked my dad, "Why are you holding her hands and kissing her?"

"What about Mommy?"

He looked at me and said, "Hey! Shut your mouth!" "You talk too much!" I stayed in silence for like an hour. I was too young to understand that he was cheating. I understood that they were friends only, but I could figure out that the way he treated my mom compared to his girlfriend was different. This did not make me happy. My Dad had a lot of girlfriends back then.

In my house, it was a different story. As soon as my parents were in the same room, my dad would start to yell and beat my mom! I didn't understand why or what she did wrong but, he would always beat her. As soon as I heard them yelling, I would run to my room and lock the door. I would go into a corner, cry, and then sing. This is how my love of singing began. I would sing loudly, trying not to hear my dad beating my Mom. There were days I would miss seeing my Dad. But I hated how he would come in and greet my brother and me so nicely and then go straight to abusing my mother at the same time. I became scared of my Dad.

When my brother and I did something bad, we would get punished. I didn't like the punishment because my Dad would yell at us at the same time. He would run and get his belt if we misbehaved. I hated getting beatings because I would get it to the point where I would have marks on my body. I also remembered at the age of eight that I did badly in school and his punishment for me was to kneel on the floor for hours. I was not allowed to stand up. If I stood up, he would get his belt and whip me again. Kneeling was so painful! He would test me and go to the store for a while. If he came back and caught me sitting down, he would take his belt and whip me.

I think the worst beating I had ever had at eight years old was when my Dad bought me new shoes and I didn't like them. My Dad was the type that if you didn't listen to what he said, he would give you a whooping! I remembered that the shoes were tan sandals. I thought they were SO ugly. I thought to myself, "Man! The kids are going to laugh at me with these sandals!" I didn't have the courage to wear those sandals, so I looked out my window from the 14th floor and threw them out! If he asked, I would tell my Dad that I lost them.

Man, that was the worst mistake ever.

He came and asked, "Where are the shoes that I bought for you?"

I said, "I can't find them!" "I lost them."

He said, "What do you mean you lost them?" "You better find them or else I'm going to beat you!" I ran downstairs from the apartment and looked thoroughly for them, and I couldn't find them. I was so scared that I couldn't go back upstairs. My Dad finally came downstairs, and he found me looking for the shoes outside. I was so scared because I saw my Dad with a belt in his hand.

He said, "If you don't find those shoes, I'm going to beat you!"

I was so embarrassed that everyone saw him yelling at me outside.

He yelled, "Where are the shoes?"

I said, "I don't know!"

He whipped me, then kicked me in my back, "Where are the shoes!"

I started crying. I was so embarrassed because the kids at the park saw how my Dad was beating me and they heard how loud I was crying. He then kicked me again in my back. He yelled and said, "Go upstairs before I kick you again!" I ran in as quickly as I could, hysterically crying. I ran straight to my room and locked the door. He finally came into the apartment and my heart was beating so loud with fear.

I heard him yelling outside my bedroom, "Ingrid!" "Ingrid!" "If you don't come out here, I'm going to break the door down and beat the hell out of you!"

I was crying hysterically and said, "Daddy please!"

I slowly came out of my room and he shouted, "Come here!"

I walked towards him, and I saw the sandals in his hands.

I thought to myself, "Oh my goodness! He found the sandals outside! Thank goodness!"

He grabbed my arm and said, "You listen to me, the next time you ever do something like this I'm going to beat the hell out of you, you understand?" "Now go put your sandals back in the box and put it in the closet.

I said, "Yes, Daddy."

I went into my room, and I did not step out for hours. My room was my comfort zone. It was a place to dream and get away from the chaos. It was my secret place. It was a place to be alone and relax. I watched TV, sang, played with the toys, and danced to my music. I loved the movie Grease during the 70s and I used to sing all their songs. I remembered attending the movie theatre with my Mom or Dad and I would love to go because of the popcorn. I used to have a crush on John Travolta because I loved him in Saturday Night Fever. I used to tell myself, "Man, I got to learn how to dance" since I concentrated more on singing. When I closed the door of my room, I would sing songs. When no one was home I would run to the record player and play the record from the movie, Saturday Night Fever. I would play the Grease record all the time. I would sing all their songs from the movie. I even remembered Diana Ross from Mahogany and sang her songs too. Yeah, I was a dreamer. If people were home, I would sing low but when no one was around I would sing loud. I was always afraid of singing in front of people even though I thought singing was fun! I always wanted to have fun. I was the one who always wanted to play outside but, not my brother. He was the one to stay indoors most of the time. He was an awesome artist though. He always loved to draw. He was good at it. I sometimes wondered how he did it. He had a vivid imagination. He sure knew how to look at something quick and just draw. We were both unique in our own ways. He had a gift, and I had a gift; we were both creative and we had to figure out how we would use our gifts in the future.

Living in New York wasn't easy, but my brother and I were rebels in our own way. I remembered my brother taking the school bus, but I don't remember the name of his school. I attended a public elementary school and I remembered walking there every day by myself. I was nine years old then. My mother would take me to school in the beginning since kindergarten but as I got older, she let me walk home alone. It's still young for a child to walk home alone but I guess my mother felt I was responsible enough to do it. It was easy to walk home because I remembered as soon as I exit the school, I had to just walk straight in one path, and I was home. There was a high school near us. I remembered there was a holiday that represented the American flag colors. I couldn't remember if it was President's Day or Independence Day but that was the day that high school students were supposed to come and beat up the students from our school. We were told anyone who's caught wearing red, white, or blue will get beat up. On that day, I was so scared because I looked at my clothes and realized I had on a blue shirt. I was so nervous that I was shaking. All the students in our school were looking at their watches or looking at the clocks around the school so they could prepare to dash home. I was waiting for the bell. Finally, it rang, and all the students ran out of their classes. As for me, I took the shortcut home. Most of the parents came and picked up their kids but, I always went home by myself, so I needed to get out of there fast! I made it home safely. I walked in and said, "Hi Mom, I'm home!" I then ran to my room and shut the door.

The next day, I went to school, and I remembered the teacher let us have recess. We would have recess every day. The teacher was outside watching while we did our activities. I painted, we played, and we even went outside. I was running around playing with my friends and went on the monkey bars, the slide, and the seesaw. While I was running around, I've noticed everyone was running away from a girl in class. She was one of the girls in our classroom who is pretty and had a crush on this Latino guy. I also thought he was cute, but I was scared to tell him and to talk to him. I was wondering why everyone was running away from her as if she had a disease. It was soon time to go in from recess, so everyone ran in quickly to their seats in the classroom. I overheard the students whispering, "She has the devil in her." "She's possessed." All the students looked scared. I didn't know what a devil was and what the word possessed meant but I assumed it must not be good. All the students sat in their seats, but many did not want to sit near her. I wasn't scared of her because I didn't see her hurt anyone. The teacher was writing on the board while we were whispering behind her back in class. I usually sit across from her so I was contemplating if I should sit there or not. I decided not to make a big deal of it, so I sat in my usual seat. Everyone was staring as they sit in their assigned seats. I noticed she took a pencil and started twirling it with her fingers while she looked in my direction since I was sitting across from her. I was a bit worried because I was wondering if she was going to take the pencil and try to stab me or even hurt herself. I didn't move a muscle. I just looked at her. I don't know why I didn't run like all the other kids did outside but, for the first time, I was curious to find out what was wrong with her. I had a piece of paper in front of me and she took the pencil and reached towards my paper and drew a small line.

I looked and said, "Hey, what is this?"

She didn't answer me. She kept looking at me with a strange smirk. Still, I didn't move away from her. She took the pencil and did it again, then gave me a smirk. I still didn't move away from her. I started to feel the warmth all over my body. It was a strange feeling. The whole class kept their distance and was still watching. She shook her head then slowly put the pencil down and backed away from me. All the students were wondering why she didn't make any sounds when she was in front of me or why she didn't get violent with me. I couldn't remember how long class was after recess, but I did remember the teacher was writing the assignment on the board and then we had to do it. We were not making a lot of noise, but we did whisper to each other. I did remember the teacher sat down most of the time while this incident with this young lady took place. Now keep in mind this was so long ago that I'm not going to remember in detail our schedule. I did remember we were not in class too long after recess.

Suddenly, the bell rang! All the students ran quickly to pick up their book bags and coats. It was time to go home. The students ran so fast to get away from her. She made a strange noise then she slowly picked up her things and left. As for me, I was the last one sitting at the table trying to figure out what I had experienced.

The teacher looked at me and said, "Ingrid, where are your parents?" "They're not coming to meet you?"

I told her I usually walk home by myself.

She said, "Ok, it's time to go home now." I got up slowly and went to pick up my things and prepared to walk home. It takes about 10-15 minutes to get home. I remembered it was one straight path. It was easy for me to get home. I used to watch all the other kids have their parents come and pick them up but, as for me, I was used to going home alone.

I think one of the reasons that I was afraid to speak up for myself as a kid was because of my Dad. He always had this look that if you talked back to him or gave him some trouble, you could tell that he was getting ready to beat you. My Dad would tell me to shut up or keep quiet. I would fear him. I would shake nervously whenever he got angry. I remembered one parent-teacher conference day at school and many of the students' parents would come. I was still nine currently. I was one of the students hoping that my parents would show up, but they never did. I was always the one in the classroom without a parent. I didn't cry but I was a little embarrassed and upset. Then one day, it was the last parents-teachers conference day before graduation for that year. I noticed that all the parents came but, there I was again, hoping that one of my parents-teachers conference day before graduation for that year. I noticed that all the parents would show up. I was just going to ask the teacher a question when suddenly my Dad came in handsome with his suit on. I yelled, "Daddy!!!" He saw me and winked and smiled. I quickly ran to him and gave him a hug. Everyone looked at us and I yelled, "This is my Daddy!!!" I was so happy. I finally felt like I wasn't left out. I was so happy that he showed up. The reason why I was so happy when my Dad showed up was that most of the time, he wasn't home. Most of the time he would sleep out. I wouldn't know his schedule. I never knew where he was. If I asked my Mom where he was, she would always answer and say she did not know.

At the meeting, the teacher announced the details about graduation day, and we were told that the girls had to wear white dresses. I remember I told my mother about graduation day and what we had to wear. It was another embarrassment for me because I didn't have a white dress. I told my mom that we needed to wear white for graduation but I guess we didn't have the money or the time. I remember she made me wear an orange dress with small white polka dots. I was so embarrassed. I was the only one who had an orange dress on and of course, I stood out among all the students. It was a disaster for me, not only because of the dress but because my parents didn't even show up to my graduation. Here we are in front of a large audience at the auditorium and I realized as I looked out when we were seated, that everyone is walking out in white and here I am walking in wearing an orange and white polka-dotted dress. I was ok after a while because I realized it was something out of my control. Strangely enough, I didn't cry but I was sad. I had a wonderful experience in elementary school but, I did have some embarrassing moments.

I always wondered why these embarrassing moments happened. You know, until this day I still have not completely figured out why I peed on myself in kindergarten and couldn't get the nerve to raise my hand to ask to go to the bathroom. Maybe, I was just not potty-trained. I used to feel like I didn't have a voice or the courage to speak up. In my family, I would be the person to always hold things in or run to my room and shut my door. I guess it was a way to shut out the world. Yep! As I have gotten older, I now understood why I couldn't speak up. I realized it was because my Mom and Dad were not really training my brother and me properly. It wasn't their fault because I realized it was just the way they were brought up. All I know is that my Mom and Dad were born in Haiti. I was a baby when I last went to Haiti. I found out that I haven't been back to Haiti because when I was a baby, I was sick. It was then that I realized I was under an attack by the Devil. Looking back at my earliest days in Haiti and knowing that I was not able to return made it clear that I was under an attack by the Devil. God had a plan, and he knew my destiny later in life.

CHAPTER 2

WHAT IS SEX?

I was sick when I was a baby in Haiti, and I have never been back since. I was born in the USA and my parents took me to visit Haiti, their home country but I became deadly ill, so they returned with me to the USA. My parents tried their best and it wasn't easy for them during the 1970s. My Dad had a lot of girlfriends but the only one I remembered was the one that I met when he took me to the amusement park and didn't bring my brother. I used to always wonder why he didn't take my brother with us to certain places, but I just figured I was Daddy's little girl.

There was a time when my brother and my mother weren't home, and I would stay in the apartment alone. She would do the same with my brother also. Sometimes my mom goes out and leaves us home alone because I guess she trusted we would be responsible, but she would always tell us not to open the door for anyone. I was still young at the time when I remember this incident I'm about to discuss. I had remembered my dad brought a woman to our house and she was older than me. I was probably about eight years old. The boy was probably two or three years older than me. I don't think my mother and my brother were home when they came over. I think they went shopping. I would have remembered seeing my brother in his room if he was home. I would've also remembered seeing my Mom if she was home. My Dad made us go in the back and play. I guess my Dad wanted to be alone with his girlfriend. I was ok I guess but I felt a little uncomfortable the fact that he's with another woman and not my Mom. He told me not to ask him questions, so I didn't. I guess this is another reason why I didn't have the courage to speak up again. Well, I ran to the back with her son and played games. We also watched T.V. and played the games like Candyland and Legos.

After a while, the boy got tired and said, "Let's go to sleep."

I said, "Why?"

He said, "We keep playing and we need a break."

I said, "Ok."

We both went under the covers and tried to sleep. I wasn't really that sleepy, but I figured why to stay up and play games when he wasn't playing the games with me. As I closed my eyes, I realized he was slowly moving his hand up and down my back.

I said, "What are you doing?"

He said, "Shhhhhhhh…" "This is a massage."

Now, keep in mind my parents had never told me about sex I didn't even know if it was a bad thing. The boy didn't hurt me, so I guessed it was okay. He slowly lifted my dress, and he just took off his pants slowly but I didn't see anything.

I turned quickly and said, "Now, what are you doing?" I quickly turned and realized he had his underwear on so of course I never saw his private parts.

He said, "Shhhhhhh… "I'm just massaging. Just keep quiet and let me practice."

I felt a little weird but then again, I didn't have the courage to tell him to stop and let's talk about what he was doing. I wasn't even sure if he was doing a bad thing. I had no idea that what we were doing was sexual. My Dad and his girlfriend were still in the other room talking. He then took his hand and felt my private parts. He was massaging. I wasn't sure what kind of massage it was, but it felt really weird. After a while of him massaging me, I thought to myself,

"How come I don't get to see his private parts and I could learn to massage?" "I didn't have the courage to say anything". I just shut my mouth and just experienced the massage.

Suddenly, we heard a noise and he whispered, "Quickly, roll up your panties.

I said, "Why?" "We'll just tell them we're massaging each other."

He said, "Just do what I tell you OK?" "We're going to get into trouble."

He quickly pulled up his pants and then told me to come to the floor and let's play Candyland.

My Dad and his girlfriend came in and said, "Ok, let's get ready so I can take you home."

I didn't get the chance to say anything, nor did I get the chance to ask the boy why we would get into trouble if I told them that we were massaging under the covers.

My Dad wanted to take his girlfriend and her son home. We got our coats and went to the car, and I sat in the back with her son. We kept talking and playing games with our dolls and toys. I didn't get the chance to ask him about the massage in the car because I remembered he said we would get into trouble. I was a little confused. I guess the massage that we did was not a good thing for us to do. I guess it was just not part of playing games. Well, the boy kept coming over with his mother when my Mom and my brother were not around, and he kept doing the massages with me. It was strange, but I took it as if it was a routine. It was my first encounter with sexuality, but I never saw his private parts and I never learned how to massage his private parts. I do not remember if I experienced an orgasm. If I did, I sure didn't know what it was at the time. It was my first experience of a guy touching my private parts. It was always his routine when he came by the house and we always kept it quiet, then one day my Dad broke up with his girlfriend. The boy stopped coming by my house. I told myself, "Ok, I guess I won't get the massage anymore."

After a while, I kind of liked the massages but didn't know if they were bad or not. I had to find out later if they were bad or not when I get the courage to ask since the boy told me to keep quiet about it. Because he didn't massage me anymore, I figured I'll do it myself since it was part of the game. I didn't know where he learned it from, but I guess the massages were not bad or I wasn't sure if it was good. All I know was it didn't feel like it was bad. I later found out it was my first encounter with sexuality.

A New Move

The next place we moved was in an area near New Jersey. I was still eight years old. My Dad decided to take my brother and me with him since he had an argument with my mom. My Dad went to one of his girlfriend's houses and he took us with him. I had to shut my mouth again because my Dad told me not to tell my Mom anything. Yup! My mother stayed and didn't come with us! I didn't have the courage to ask him anymore because I would've gotten a slap in the mouth. I wasn't a big fan of living in this state because his girlfriend was quite mean to me and her relative was there also and he wasn't nice. They were nice in the beginning when I came but after a while, they started to be mean to me.

I didn't like this friend of his because she was mean. She took advantage of her meanness. I guess she felt since we were staying in her house, she has the right to treat my brother and me any way she wanted. Her mother lived upstairs, and she was nice. If I wanted to go and talk, I would go right upstairs and visit her. My father's girlfriend's relative was a different story. I didn't like him because he would scream at us if we didn't do what he said. I think he thought he could get away with doing whatever he wanted because he was the relative of my Dad's girlfriend. There were times that he would have his dog attack us. I didn't like that. The dog wasn't mean all the time but once his master said, "Sic him!" the dog will obey.

I couldn't remember every little thing, but I did remember some good times. The best part I remembered was that my best friend at the time lived down the block. I remembered I had another friend who lived across the street. These were the two main people I remembered the most. When I would come from school, I would quickly ask if I could go outside and play. Spending time with them allowed me to get away from the horrible relative of my father's girlfriend. He was an asshole. If you didn't do what he says he would hit, you. I know for me I didn't have the courage to open my mouth much and even if I ever tried to hit him, I know that he was stronger than me.

There is one real reason why I hated him so much. Since I did not have the courage to fight him, at nine years old he took sexual advantage of me. He would yell at me whenever he asks me to do something, and I would refuse to do it. Every time I refuse, he would then ask me to take off my clothes. If I didn't do it, he would hit me. He would always do this to me when no one was home. He would always do this when I get home from school while my father and his girlfriend went to work. I hated every moment of it. He would get on top of me. He never penetrated me so I guess what they would call it is a dry hump. He was young and so was I, but he was older than me. I would yell at him and tell him to stop but he was stronger, and he would hit me. I always felt helpless. It became a routine. He was the one in charge of babysitting. I would hate the way he would yell at me to take off my clothes. I hated the way that I was so helpless. I hated the way how I couldn't win against him to fight back. I hated the way that he couldn't just leave me alone. I later realized this was rape. Then one day, we got caught. He had me take off all my clothes and he had his top on. He started to get on top of me then suddenly, we heard the door. I didn't hear the car in the driveway so that was weird. He hurriedly jumped off me and threw on his pants and ran into the basement. I was trying to hurry up and get dressed but it was too late. It was my Dad. He came quickly down the stairs and came right into my room and checked on me. He realized I had no clothes on.

He said, "Hey, what's happening here?" "Why do you have no clothes on?"

I was such in a state of shock that I couldn't say anything, I didn't have a voice. I couldn't think of anything to say. I should have said I just took a shower or something, but I couldn't even think of that!

He said, "I'm going to ask you again, why you don't have no clothes on?"

I just told him I was getting dressed.

He said, "Put your clothes on before I beat you!"

I said, "Yes, Daddy."

My Dad quickly went into the basement room and found him in there, without most of his clothes on.

My Dad said, "What are you doing here?"

He said, "I was just cleaning my room."

My Dad grabbed him and pulled him out of the room and said, "Get upstairs and put your clothes on!"

He came back to my room and told me to get upstairs too. My heart was pounding like crazy. My mind was racing, wondering what punishment I was about to receive. It was a horrible experience. My Dad went and told his girlfriend what happened and all I could hear from a distance was her yelling, "WHAT???" I could tell she was not used to hearing about her relative doing anything bad. Well, in the end, my Dad beat me with the belt. His girlfriend yelled at her relative and hit him too. I was smiling when he got hit because he really deserved it. He took advantage of me. As for me, I haven't done anything wrong. I was the victim, but I didn't have the courage or the strength to fight back. I was so angry at myself because I didn't say anything. I was also so angry at my Dad because he hit me as if I was the blame. I didn't start the incident, but I guess the fact that I got involved made things uncomfortable for him. I hated myself for not being strong enough to fight back. I also hated myself for not having the voice to defend myself.

I was thinking to myself, "What was I afraid of?" "Was I afraid of people not liking me?" "Was I afraid of the consequences if I did say something?" It took me a long time to learn to open my mouth and say something.

Once, when I was in fifth grade, I had a teacher named Mrs. Fardi, I would always come to class and do my work. One day, I had to take the reading and math test. I was pretty good at math, but I wasn't good at reading. Fifth grade was the grade you needed to pass in order to get to the next school year. If you didn't pass both the reading and the math test, you would get left-back and must repeat the grade. I remembered my challenge was that I hated reading. I didn't have the patience to sit and read the whole chapter. I would be very good at reading aloud in class. I used to be in the spelling bee, so I was pretty good at figuring out words. My challenge was not reading the paragraphs my challenge was understanding what I've just read; it was the comprehension. I was not good under pressure. When we had to take the test, I hated the fact that for the reading we were being timed.

In the end, I passed the math test but failed the reading. Mrs. Fardi called me after class when everyone went home. She told me, "Ingrid, you are one of my best students but I'm so sorry to say that you did not pass the reading test so you're going to have to get left-back." I was so angry. I broke down and cried. I told Mrs. Fardi that I cannot go home and tell my parents the news.

She said, "Ingrid, you're going to have to tell your parents and the only way you will pass is if you take the test all over again." In other words, I had to take the makeup exam. I was so scared to tell my Dad because I knew he was going to beat me. I don't like to get beatings by my Dad. I remembered there were maybe three other students in the class that didn't pass either. My best friend and I walked home, and we both looked at our report cards. It wasn't bad except I didn't pass the reading and I didn't pass to the next grade. As we walked home, I remembered my best friend, comforting me saying, "Don't worry Ingrid, just tell your parents and go to summer school and take the test over so you can be with us in the next grade. I was crying hysterically and still didn't feel reassured. Finally, my best friend made it to her house, and I was going to ask her if I could stay with her but, I had to go home and tell my parents. Again, I still didn't have the guts. I still didn't have the courage. I still didn't open my mouth. As I got to the front of the house, I asked myself if I was ready for a beating. I went into the house. I noticed my brother was home. My Dad wasn't home yet and of course, his girlfriend's relative was there but of course, I wasn't going to tell him anything since I hated him. I ran downstairs to my room and hid the report card. I sat in my room thinking, "Boy, I really did not want to go to summer school because I didn't want to take the reading test again since I hated reading.

Later, my father's girlfriend and my father's girlfriend's relative were home. I was praying and hoping that they wouldn't notice that it was the last day of school and we had received our report cards. Finally, my brother opened his big fat mouth to show off that he had good grades and passed. As for me, I kept quiet until my Dad asked me for my report card.

I said, "You know, Dad, I didn't receive it?"

He said, "What? What do you mean you didn't receive it?"

I said, "The teacher asked us to stay after class since she felt we were good students. Maybe she didn't finish entering the grades yet."

Boy, I lied, and I buried myself into a deeper hole. I couldn't believe it. I finally had the courage to say something, but it wasn't good. It was a lie. My Dad just took the answer as if it was normal and he just mentioned letting him know when I received it. Oh boy! Now, the report card hung over my head every day. Every time I went into my room, I would look at the report card and then put it back in its hiding spot. Summer was beginning and obviously, you can tell my mind was made up for not attending summer school. I didn't want to miss the fun of hanging out. Every day I would think about how Mrs. Fardi kept pressuring me to tell my parents so they can enroll me in summer school. I still didn't have the courage or the voice to tell them.

Summer passed and I realized my Dad never asked me again about the report card. When school started, I had to face everyone, and they had to see that I repeated 5th grade. On the first day of school, I returned home normally I realized my Dad was home early. I didn't know what was going on. I walked in and said, "Hi Dad,"

He said, " Get on your knees and stay there until I tell you to move." My heart was pounding, and I was trying to figure out what happened. He ran downstairs and returned with my report card. My heart dropped! I was thinking to myself how does he find it?" My Dad told me that my teacher called and wanted to meet for a parent-teacher conference to discuss my studies. My Dad was so angry when he found out that I had been left-back and didn't tell him. Oh Boy! I was in for it! I was forced to remain on my knees and not move. He said, that if I moved a muscle or went to another room, he would beat me very badly. My Dad went out and didn't come back for hours! Can you imagine staying on your knees without moving a muscle? Of course, I snuck a couple of times to sit down but it was the worst punishment ever. I finally heard the car in the driveway, and he came in and slammed the door. My Dad went right into his room and grabbed the belt and pulled my arm up.

He said, "Get up!"

I yelled, "Daddy, please!"

He said, "Get up!"

He beat me with the belt so much I lost count of how many lashes I received. All I remembered the next day, were the whelps on my back and arms. I was thinking to myself if I ever have kids, I wouldn't beat them like my Dad. Well, my punishment continued after that beating. My Dad wanted to see me read a book every time he arrived home. I was good at math because my Dad taught me. He realized how slow I was in getting the answers so he would beat me. I became a math whiz. As far as the reading, it took me a long time to figure out. I used to think of myself as being slow. I would read aloud but my Dad wouldn't ask me comprehension questions, he just wanted to hear me read. I started to ask my friends for help with understanding the books that I was reading. I would read but not grasp the information.

A good friend of mine said to me, "You have to read as if you are telling a story." "When someone tells you a story you understand right?"

I said, "Yes,"

She said, "Ok, read to me as if you're telling a story. I looked at the paragraphs and I felt overwhelmed because of the number of words but as I read it aloud like a story, it all made sense. She then asked me questions.

She said, "Ok who are the characters?" "What was the main idea?" "What do you think is the title of this paragraph?" "What is paragraph two about?"

I got all the answers right. I figured out; read as if you're telling a story. It took me a while to really get into enjoying reading. Now,

I just pick up a book and skim or read quickly to get through the paragraphs because I realized I didn't have the patience to sit and read and absorb. I realized I wasn't patient enough for it. Even today, I still don't have the patience for it. I love magazines, especially if it contains my interests or how-to books. I'm quick to just skim and move on.

Moving Again

One day, I came home from school, and I remembered my Dad was telling me to pack my things. I told myself oh boy! Dad is moving again. I guess things didn't work out with his girlfriend. I wasn't sure if they had an argument or was it because she did not want my brother and me there anymore. All I remember was that my father's girlfriend's mother was not happy. She cried when she saw us leaving. I was wondering if we were going to move to another one of his girlfriend's houses, but I realized we were going someplace else. Yup! I found out later, that things did not work out with his girlfriend and so we were forced to move. I don't know in detail how it happened but with her personality, I wouldn't be surprised if she told him to get out of her house in the end.

Every summer, my brother and I would visit our relatives in the northeast. I have a lot of relatives. It was a lot of fun because there were also kids living there. I started to understand little by little where the whole moving thing took place. It was instilled in me. My Dad moved around so much when we were young that I guess I adapted it from him. I just didn't like how he would have different girlfriends. It became a trend. He would have a girlfriend and move in with them and we would move with him too while my mother stayed back in the apartment alone. My Mom wouldn't know all this because my Dad wouldn't tell her.

This time, the move was a little different because we were on our way to the northeast. It was a place to hang around with my cousins because every summer we would have a blast! When I found out that my brother and I were going to move to the northeast full time, everyone started jumping up and down. My cousins were awesome! One of them was like my sister and we got along so well. Later, when I moved into the house, I found out she didn't live there anymore. I was sad, but it was ok because I had my other cousins.

This moving journey involved me living with other family members that I eventually started to get to know. I remember that the neighborhood was nice, but the house was dim. I didn't like that the house was dim but, I adjusted because there were lamps and light switches anyway. I just wished the house had some brightness. It was still a cool house to live in since many relatives instead of moving into my father's girlfriend's house. Here we go off to another area!

CHAPTER 3

WELCOME TO THE NORTH-EAST

Every summer, my Dad would take my brother and me to visit my cousins in the northeast. My cousin from my uncle's side was there and my cousin from my aunt's brother's side was there. At the time, Grand'Mere (which means Grandmother in French) also lived there. I even had a chance to meet my Godmother and my cousin from Louisiana who used to live there also. Whew! It was a funhouse when my brother and I would go every summer. It was a full house! There were cousins who I stayed with who were like my brothers and sisters. My aunts and uncles were like my parents. I had a lot of aunts and uncles! When my Dad decided to move us to my aunt's house, I was sad because I didn't see my other cousin who I used to play games with. I later realized it was ok because at least I had a blast hanging with the other cousins. We would always do crazy stuff together.

The house was so full, but we had space for pets. We had cats, dogs, and fish! I think we even had a bird. For the most part, we got along with each other though, of course, there were days where we had fights but what family wouldn't have that? It wouldn't be normal if we never had fights. I remembered we used to jump up and down on the bed and call ourselves our favorite superheroes. We used to take our towels and put them on our backs like capes. We would jump off the bed and jump up and down as if we were acting like we were flying. We would make so much noise that my aunt would yell from the top of her lungs! She would give us a warning a couple of times, but we still managed to have a lot of fun! It was awesome!

My aunt would ask my Dad to stop by and give her money to help support my brother and me but after a while, he stopped. My Dad would come to visit but after a while, he visited less and less. I started to wonder what happened. It felt like he just abandoned us. My aunt was not happy about that because she felt that it should be a duty for a father to support their child. I didn't know where he lived so I had no more information on him. My aunt didn't know either, so she decided to just continue to take care of us. I must thank GOD for that because we would have been sent to a foster home. I then realized we were not going back to my Mom's house anymore. I haven't heard from her, and I haven't connected with her because we had no information to connect with her anymore. It was time to just start accepting that this will be my new home. It was the beginning of another exciting time since my brother, and I loved coming over to our aunt's house.

I was so happy to live with my family in the beginning because I loved the way we were the popular family of the block. I remembered my neighbors on the block. Next door, we had the coolest friends. One of my cousins had a best friend and they hung with each other a lot. They had so many similarities that you would think they are brothers. The only difference is that he was from another country. The neighbors on the other side of us were cool too. They had a daughter and a son. They were always friendly with us. The other neighbors who lived across the street were from Colombia. We had people from China and even Ecuador living on our street as well! We even had people from Italy. Most of the people that lived on the next block were African Americans. We lived on a block that had a diversity of people, then the next block would be all Black people and then the next block after that would be all White. It was an interesting setup.

I used to hang around with some wonderful girls that went to junior high school with me. They were an awesome crew. It was fun hanging out with them. Sometimes we would walk home together. One of my closest friends lived around the corner from me and she passed away. She had a disease, and it wasn't curable at the time. I remembered she made all of us get together and hang out and it felt a little uncomfortable because it was as if she knew when she was going to die. When she passed away, I cried for days. I was so sad because I couldn't believe that she was gone. I told her one day we will meet again. RIP my good friend!

The people in my neighborhood were cool but I loved hanging with the fellas. My cousins, of course, had guy friends so I was able to meet them. I was in junior high school during this time, so I was probably 13 years old. I couldn't stop laughing because every time the guys got together, they would do some crazy stuff and you had no choice but to laugh. I had my crushes also. I used to have a crush on this guy who lived down the block. I knew it would not be easy to date any of these guys because they were really close with my cousins. It was as if there was a sign on me that said "don't cross the sister" zone. It was interesting because people dated each other anyway. It's too much to name who dated who but, it was funny to find out who liked who.

My first kiss was with a guy who lived around the corner from me. He's going down in my history book as the first guy who kissed me. Later, I took the risk to sneak and date the other guys. I had my crushes with guys in school and in my neighborhood. The one who I took a risk to have as my boyfriend was the one who lived up the block. When we see each other today, we are still cool with one another. He can still make me laugh though he's happily married. I'm proud of him on that note.

Now, about the pets, I had forgotten a funny incident about the pets in our home. We used to have fish and the fish tank was in the dining room. We also had other cousins who would stop by and visit our house. My aunt had many other family members who would come by and visit. My aunt had one cousin who had three kids: one older son, a daughter, and a younger son. They were also cool cousins! We had so much fun but there was an incident that I cannot forget. It wasn't that funny because the fish died in the process, but it is hilarious to think about it now. I don't know who did the deed, but it was shocking that it took place. I remembered I quickly went upstairs and when I came downstairs the fish were floating at the top of the fish tank. I was surprised so I turned to one of my relatives and said, "Ooooooooh, someone is going to get into trouble…"

I asked, "What happened?" She said, "Well, someone put the dishwashing liquid in the fish tank.

She told me the person thought the soap would clean out the tank. The person felt that the tank was dirty. I was trying hard not to laugh but at the same time, I was so shocked and sad. It was sad to see the fish floating at the top of the tank! I know the person didn't mean any harm, but I knew when my aunt came home from work that she was going to be angry. Well, it happened! She came home and noticed the fish were dead and she was mad. Of course, she had to tell their father what they did. Strangely enough, I don't remember who did it. I only remembered that one of my cousins told me the story of how it happened. I know I told a few of my close friends and they started laughing because it was a crazy incident. In the end, we decided to buy more fish with a clean tank.

We also had other pets. We had a cat that was black and had beautiful eyes. It was one of my cousin's favorite pets. I think even until this very present day the cat is still alive. The last pet I remembered we had was a dog. He was a Chow Chow mixed. He had fluffy hair. He was an interesting dog. He was adorable but he had an attitude at times. The dogs were always kept in the backyard since the doghouse was located there. All the dogs we had would stay in the doghouse. I loved all the dogs we had. He was awesome but he passed away. I remember my cousin started crying. I was so sad to hear her upset.

I asked, "What's wrong?"

She said, "The dog died! He's in the backyard! She found out that he died when she woke up that morning and went to the kitchen, looked out the window, and noticed he was lying flat on the ground.

I ran outside the backyard and saw the dog lying flat on the ground. I started to tear up also. I was thinking to myself there goes another dog. We were told it's normal because certain breeds last a certain time. I think he had a heart attack, or he was sick. We were all sad! On a happier note, we got another dog, and he was funny! I remember my uncle would call him a dopey dog. I think it was because whenever we asked him to do something, he would do things the opposite. He was also another mixed breed. He looked like half Doberman and half Beagle because of his ears. He was black, white, and brown. I thought he was cute. I used to always love to hug him.

There was another funny incident that the whole family had to laugh about because of what the dog did. One time, one of my cousins ordered pizza. We had the pizza delivered to our house, I remembered the pizza man came and we paid him, and we put the pizza on the kitchen counter. I remembered opening the pizza and it looked scrumptious. I ran upstairs to call everyone to come to eat because the pizza had arrived. Everyone came running downstairs looking forward to eating the pizza. Suddenly, one of my cousins opened the flap and found there was no cheese on the pizza!

I looked and said, "That's impossible! I saw the pizza looked in order."

The cheese was gone but the crust was the only thing left in the box. The only thing I could think of was the dog!!! I yelled for him! The dog was hiding somewhere. It had to be the dog because it wasn't that long that I turned away to call everyone to come to eat. I couldn't believe it! Some of us laughed but some of us were shocked to realize that he ate only the cheese from the pizza and left the rest! My Uncle came home and said, "What a dopey dog!" I don't remember beating him or punishing him, but I do remember he got into trouble.

We had some funny pets! Most of the pets we had were adorable and funny! We had a lot of fun playing with them. He stood out the most because he did some funny stuff!

I remembered there was another incident where one of my cousins just bought new boots. He lived with us also. I remember he was not a big fan of pets, but he adjusted. One day, he came home from work and went into his room and yelled, "Who did this to my boots?" I remember running upstairs and seeing a chunk was bitten off at the heel of one of his boots. He was so upset because they were brand new. I looked at the boots and said to him who else would have done this? It was the dog. My Uncle came home and found out what he did, and he just said, "What a dopey dog." Yep! He was known as the dopey dog. We went through a couple of pets, but this one took the cake. As far as the cats, I remembered there was another one and he was grey with black stripes. One thing about him was that he was fierce in catching birds. Sometimes we would get up in the morning and realize that he had a bird in his mouth. He was also quick in catching mice. When in doubt and you wanted to kill a mouse, get one of the cats near the area and they scooped them out. Our cats were awesome for that. We had a fabulous time with our pets because there was something unique about each one of them. I felt that each of the pets had a job to keep the house intact.

If I had to choose a pet, I would get a dog. I love dogs. My favorite dog of all the ones we had was a German Shepherd. I remembered teaching her how to sit, lay down, and give me paw and come. I had fun training her and she was lovable. She later got hit by a car. I was devastated. I cried because she was my sidekick. When she got hit, the vet couldn't do much to get her back up again. They had to put her to sleep. I was sad. I wasn't sure if I wanted to see another pet in our house again. The cats are a little sneaky, but I came to find out that I'm allergic to cats. I am quick to sneeze around the cats. I like pets but I love the dogs most when they're puppies. Oh, the puppies are so cute! My cousin went and bought turtles. I think they were snapping turtles. It was awesome to see them in action.

What I loved most about living in the Northeast were the family dinners we had every weekend. I also loved when my friends would stop by the house. We had a lot of friends of my cousins who would stop by the house but, I had wonderful friends who GOD put into my life to move me into His direction. It was not an accident as to how we all met each other. My aunt is an excellent cook. Everyone around the neighborhood knew she was awesome in the kitchen. We always had friends who would stop by every Sunday because it was family dinner time. Family dinner time reminded me of the movie Soul Food. My aunt would cook dinner every Sunday like it was Thanksgiving. I used to love helping her cook because it gave me a chance to watch her. She was good at cooking the food, but she would always ask me to help prepare the food like season the meat or prepare the table. From all my years of moving from place to place, hands down my aunt was the best cook of Haitian food. People would tell her that she should open a Haitian restaurant. There are so many Haitian dishes she would make. The popular dishes in Haiti were black rice, rice and beans, rice and peas, banan pesse (which was fried flat plantain), legumes, rice with bean sauce, fish, chicken, and steak, to name a few. There were even quick dishes like Maii Mune (it's corn but it looks like cream of wheat) that she could turn into something delicious. One normally ate the Maii Mune with bean sauce and smoked fish. Her soups were popular also, especially the pumpkin and vegetable soups. My favorite meat was the oxtails but today I stay away from red meat and just eat fish and chicken now.

In Haiti, I was told by my aunt that when people are poor they would eat Akasan with bread and cheese for breakfast. Man! It was my favorite breakfast meal! Akasan is like a cornmeal but very fine in order to drink it. You just have one cup with bread and cheese and you're already full. Even today, whenever I visit my Haitian friends, I always ask if they can make Akasan. If I had to choose my favorite rice meal it would be the black mushroom rice. We call it Diri ak Djon Djon. To make it one must take black mushrooms from Haiti and boil it in water which gives the water its black color. The flavor is nice. One of my Haitian friends told me that you can also buy Maggie cubes which are black, and you can also use that to color the water, which will also make black rice but that's a fast way. The mushroom is a longer process because you must boil the mushroom. The plantains were another favorite of mine because I loved the sweet ones. I used to love how my aunt would make the plantains with sauce. It's good with rice and beans and chicken. I will admit that I miss my aunt's cooking, but the only thing is that the food is very fattening. It's delicious but you can gain weight easily. The food is rich like Spanish food. Rice and meat were the main dishes all the time with Haitian food. I visited Haitian restaurants in New York, but I still feel that no one can top my aunt's cooking. I still wished that she opened a Haitian restaurant. She would have a lot of customers. Everyone in our neighborhood loved my aunt's cooking. It was always interesting to hear some of the neighbors stop by and ask if my aunt cooked for the day! The routine would be that she would get up in the morning, attend church and then come home and start the Sunday meals.

High School

I had other good friends that loved to come by also. They were awesome. I attended Edward R. Murrow High School. I remembered it was located right around the corner from the NBC studios. It was awesome because our school was known for broadcasting. I wouldn't be surprised if interns attended the set at the studio. I loved Edward R. Murrow High School! Some high schools called it periods on their schedules, but we called it Bands. A Band, B Band, C Band etc. The Cosby Show and the soap opera, Another World used to be filmed right around the corner. During lunchtime or on our breaks my friends and I would sneak out and try to visit the studio to see if any of the actors would come outside. Yep! I was one of those fans! I was always surrounded by people in the Entertainment Industry because I had dreams of getting into the business. I did a lot of extra work in films, real people model work, and auditioned for hip-hop dancing and singing. I've met so many entertainers in the business I can't even keep count.

When I did extra work for films, I would meet the actors on the set. They were nice on the set though. My other best friend, Selah, would attend auditions on a regular. Now in high school, I had some very talented friends. I had a group of girls that I hung out with, and we called ourselves Elite. God brought us together. We were Salome, Tamar, Esther, Selah, Sarai, Naomi, Anna, and Ruth. Priscilla and Gomer were also part of the group when we had our talent show. We had gotten popular when we participated in the talent show.

Ms. Fire was in charge, and she was an awesome teacher. She was like a mentor to us. One thing I remembered about Ms. Fire was that she always wanted us as Blacks to become independent. I remembered she would always want us to work together because that was the problem with the African Americans in our community. There was always some fight taking place and she would always tell us that we needed to stop fighting, work together, and progress as a community. As I've gotten older, I understood the whole purpose now. This continues to be a big problem in our communities. We need to get along and work together so we can build big businesses. As African Americans, we can go far if we just unite and work together. We have so much talent as a people, and we can really fly high and soar when we work together as a team. The enemy would want us to fight so we wouldn't be productive. We have come a long way as people of color, and we need to keep going. Ms. Fire would always want us to encourage one another, uplift one another, and support each other as a team so things would run smoothly. As students of the Communication Arts, we will always remember Ms. Fire for that. It was an incredible high school. I met so many wonderful friends and there are a lot of them that are very successful today. The group members in Elite are still my friends today.

One other group that I was part of was Simply Mystique. Two members, Denise, and Michele attended the same high school. Murrow was a unique school. I guess they did things a little differently than other high schools. It wasn't a school where everyone would just get in easily, you had to be picked. I still have no idea until now how they chose their students for the school. The best part was meeting my good friends from high school. They were all Christ-centered. They loved the Lord and we always spoke about GOD. I even remembered visiting their churches. We all were from different denominations, but we followed Christ. It was important to us because we realized with God in our lives, we succeeded in everything. We learned to have a relationship by learning about the Lord and following His ways. I loved the fact that my friends were Godly women. I've witnessed some wonderful testimonies in their lives. Even if they went through some tough trials, they still followed the Lord. I was brought up to believe in God. I still do and I'm so glad God is with me to meet some friends in high school and have the experience to attend a popular TV program, called the Arsenio Hall Show! It was the highlight of my high school life!

CHAPTER 4

FLAVA OF THE FUTURE CONTEST: ARSENIO HALL!

Simply Mystique was an Acapella group that I was a part of. The name represented elegance. We had a wonderful time together. What really made us popular was our amazing experience at the Arsenio Hall Show. We were at the Flava of the Future Contest on November 19, 1993. When we were in high school, I, along with two friends, Esther and Dee from my group attended the Gospel Chorus. I think we looked forward to the gospel chorus in school. Our gospel chorus teacher was inspiring. We had some interesting teachers and they really prepared us for our dreams. Now, during the time of our high school years, The Arsenio Hall Show was very popular. Simply Mystique was a group put together by Michele Gittens. Her sister Denise and brother Michel were also involved. The group members were Lennon Edwards, Roberto Joseph, Denise Gittens-Duliepre, Michele Gittens, Michel Gittens, and Sandy Howell-Crosson. We also had other group members that would come and go. God was in control. We were also all Catholic. I later attended another Christian University, so I no longer practiced Catholicism. The group became my other family. We would rehearse so many times a week. It was also my way to vent my frustrations. I loved to sing! We were good singers, and we had a unique style about us. We were elegant and classy so that's how we came up with the name Simply Mystique! I remembered Arsenio announced on TV a call for people to send in the videotapes of their talent to enter a contest called Flava of the Future Contest. We figured, let's give it a try! The beauty of our group was that we are Christians and we always believed with God all things are possible! Our group would attend church every Sunday and we would always pray before rehearsals and pray for each other all the time. We got along so well that we were really like brothers and sisters.

We decided to enter the contest, so we got together and filmed ourselves singing. We sent in the tape, and we got selected! I was so happy! We were all jumping for joy! We were even in the Daily Newspaper. We were so excited! We all prayed and asked God to guide us and prepare us for this show. The word started to spread of course and, in my mind, I was so happy because I wanted to sing, act and dance. This would get us all in to demonstrate our talents.

It was an awesome experience, but it was also a reality check about what Hollywood was all about. We were flown to L.A. and got put in a hotel. It was nice. We all had the chance to see what L.A. looked like as we drove towards the hotel. L.A. looked like a cool city to me and what grabbed my attention the most were the palm trees. When we arrived at the hotel and checked, we had to make sure we made some time to rehearse. We prepared our outfits. What did we wear? We wore clothes that were elegant and classy that would fit the name of our group. The women wore black dresses while the men wore tan shirts, black vests, and black pants. They looked sharp! The ladies looked beautifully elegant! We were nervous but at the same time excited about where this journey was going to take us. It was our dream to one day sign a record deal and be the next Boys II Men! Boyz II Men is a very talented group. We admired how they got together and rehearsed. They had such a unique sound, especially an Acappella. It takes skill to really sing and harmonize Acappella. I know I was thinking about their style as we rehearsed before we were to go on.

We met Arsenio when he stopped by to see us. He was so cool; I loved the fact that he was so down to earth. Sometimes, you meet celebrities, and they have an attitude. I usually pray for them and keep it moving. We had a chance to receive an autographed picture from him which was cool. I think we took a picture with him, but I don't remember if it was with our camera or theirs. It was in the 90s when this took place, so I know times have changed with technology. Arsenio gave us encouragement and what I loved about his talk with us was that he incorporated God into it.

Everything was so fast-paced! He had a make-up crew, wardrobe, and people working on the set. We even had sound checks which were important. Everything went so fast that I didn't remember ever having the chance to explore L.A. I just remembered that this was a competition and we had to find out who was going to win first prize. If you win first prize, you will receive a record contract. The other contestants were nice! Each of them had different talents. I can't remember all their names, but I remember there was a female singer, a rapper, a country singer, a male singer, a girl group, and our acapella group. The three contestants I remembered were Joanne Penneck, Tonedeff, and Delious Kennedy. Tonedeff was friendly. All the contestants were friendly and at the same time, we wished each other luck. Without the group, we prayed. We believed if God was for us who can be against us. I had to also remember no matter what happens God was in control. If he wanted us to win, then it was meant to be. If not, God had a different purpose.

Well, each contestant went out and performed, and soon it was our turn to walk on the stage Arsenio gave us a quick talk. He wanted us to believe in ourselves and what we represented. I wonder if Arsenio noticed we looked scared or nervous. I know I was nervous because what went through my mind were the viewers watching and if we made a mistake, it would be on record forever. They called our group to come to the stage. I made a mistake because I forgot to say my part before we get into the song. I remembered I was supposed to say, "Here we go!" and I couldn't believe I had forgotten my part. I kept on going and again I knew it was my nervousness that took over. As for the rest of us, we sang beautifully throughout the rest of the song.

We saw the judges and one of the judges was Johnny Gill! I was so happy because he was an awesome singer. The other judges were from different radio stations from different states. I rooted for Tonedeff because he was nice. He went out and rapped an original piece. I remembered Joanne Penneck because she sang a Whitney Houston song. I love Whitney Houston! I remembered I would buy all her albums and just sing along. The contestant that blew me away was Delious Kennedy. He sounded like Johnny Gill. He had a very strong voice, and it was beautiful. The other contestant who did country was pretty good too! The girl group was talented, and I remembered they were from Atlanta! Suddenly, it was judging time! I knew our group was praying and it felt like if it is God's will so be it. No matter what happened, blessed be the name of the Lord. I remembered the judges made their tally and Johnny Gill went up to Arsenio with the winners. I heard our names, and we came in second place with Joanne Penneck. There was a tie! I was shocked! When Arsenio announced first place, I was nervous! He announced Delious Kennedy! I was not surprised because his sound was awesome! I was thinking to myself that they had to be looking for a certain person. We were the only acapella group, so we were pretty good. The beauty of all this was that we all had a chance to showcase our talents on national television and have a taste of a little fame.

All the other contestants were still content, and we shook hands and congratulated Delious. I was proud of him because he later became a member of the group ALL FOR ONE! Their hit song was "I Swear." The album came out in 1993. I was so happy to hear that because I was curious about what he would end up doing. It was told to us that the first prize would be a record contract. I didn't know that it would ask Delious to join a group, but it was a good foot in the door for him. He sounded so good that I felt that he could just get a record deal on his own. When I saw ALL FOR ONE video, I was happy to see Delious and say, "Hey! I met that guy!" I've met so many people in the entertainment business, so it was a time to continue in it. As far as the other contestants, I don't know where they are now but at least we all had a chance to taste a bit of fame.

I always wanted to get into the entertainment business. I didn't care how I would get in as long as I just got myself involved in something. I believed so much in Simply Mystique because we were all talented in some way. God gave us a talent and we used it. After the show, we were on talk shows and radio shows. We were on 98.7 KISS in New York, we were on WBLS in New York, and CD 101.9. We were also on the Charles Perez show. The show was later canceled but it was a good experience to be on it. Simply Mystique was hoping that we would get a record deal after our experience, but it wasn't easy. People had heard of us but, there was always something. We had a manager, and her name was Janice Gordon and she was good friends with Michele from our group. We tried different record companies. The record companies sure heard of us, but the problem was that they wanted to meet us within their terms. I didn't meet with the record companies personally, but we received the reports from our manager and our group member, Michele.

The only record company I had a chance to meet were people from

Motown Records. I met Mike Bivins from Biv 10 Records in the elevator because I used to work for UPS. It was cool because he was one of the members of New Edition! I love New Edition! I've met Mike Bivins and Johnny Gill! Awesome! I remembered one time I heard that New Edition was going to be at Tower Records. My best friend, Selah came with me, and we were in the store a bit hoping to see New Edition come in. They later made an announcement for us to leave the store if we were not buying anything. We went out and from outside of Tower Records we looked through the window. I remembered Selah was right next to me and I said to her, "Remember when you see New Edition come towards us don't scream ok?"

She said, "Ok." Here comes New Edition and what happens? Selah screamed my ears off! Got to love your best friend! I remembered seeing all the ladies on top of cars even on top of mailboxes, screaming and it was crazy! My favorite group member was Ralph Tresvant! I'll admit it! I was excited about seeing the group. It was so cool seeing them walking in so calmly in the store while we were all outside screaming our heads off! So, when I met Mike Bivins, it reminded me of how much we loved New Edition.

Motown Records was one of our stops to pick up and drop off packages from UPS. Some record companies wanted to change our image, some wanted to change our name, and some wanted to change the members in our group. I realized that the members of our group were not happy at all. We've worked so hard to get our name and image that it just wouldn't make sense to change. We wanted to have a clean image. To change the group members would mean we would have to change our family and we were not ready for that. We loved Boys II Men because they had a clean image. They didn't come across as raunchy! We were hoping we could be the next acapella group like them but be a mixed-gender group. God was the center of our lives, and we were not about to change and cross over. We wanted to be a gospel R&B group. I wasn't happy when I heard a record company wanted to change group members. We've been with each other so long that we decided we wanted to stay as family.

I was happy that we didn't sign a contract at the start of the process because we would have to accept some of their terms. I would hear stories of how people didn't care what it took to get a record deal. It's sad to hear some of the things some record companies would force you to do if you wanted a record deal that badly. It was like selling your soul to the Devil. God saved us from signing contracts. I even remembered Mrs. Gittens would always say to us, "No one is signing any record contracts." At the time I wanted to just get my foot in the door, but God protected me. I didn't see it at the time but later I understood why. God had a different purpose for me.

Simply Mystique decided to do things differently. We decided to take matters into our own hands. We decided to have our own record label and make our own album. Our first project was a Christmas album. We were able to do things on our own and make our own decisions. It wasn't easy to make an album because it costs money. We weren't rich but at least our names were known to the public for a bit. It had to be promoted. We prayed and asked God to give us a chance to do an album.

The project was successful. The songs on the album were beautiful. It started with an Intro spoken by Sugar Crosson. Sugar also did "The New Year's Countdown!" The song, "Carol of the Bells" was beautifully sung by Michele and Sandy. The song, "The First Noel" was sung by Sandy. The song, "Simply Christmas" was sung by Denise and Michelle. There was a song written by Lennon Edwards called, "If it doesn't snow." It was an original. I wrote and sang a song called,

"Join the celebration!" Michel and Michelle did the arrangement for "Silent Night." The song, "Brand New Year" and "The Christmas poem" was from all of us. We even had a "Brand New Year" acapella remix. We even invited Jay "Mixin" Dixon from 98.7 KISS FM radio station to participate in our album. He did the Christmas Request Line! We had a blast doing the album!

It was a success for all of us to write, produce and sing on the album and we did it all ourselves. We were so proud of ourselves for this success. We got the album, so we performed in different places. It was even played on the radio stations. We even had a chance to sing a slogan for KISS FM in New York. "Season's Greetings from Simply Mystique" was the name of the slogan played during Christmas on KISS FM.

I remembered they played one of our songs every time behind Boys II Men. I had dreams of meeting them one day, but I haven't had the chance yet. The album was our style. Even to this present day, if I had the chance to meet Boys II Men, I would be very happy. I would love to hear them sing live also. When the album got on the radio, we had the chance to be interviewed on KISS FM. We did a few performances. One experience I remembered was singing for The Salvation Army. We saw a man dressed as Santa Claus in the street ringing his bell with a bucket in his hand, asking for donations. It was his turf, but we asked him if he wouldn't mind if we helped him raise some money since it was for a good cause. Our goal was just to promote our album and get noticed. We didn't want the money. As we performed, we saw a crowd start to form. Santa Claus was happy because he was able to raise a lot of money to help the needy. We sang one of our songs from the album "Carol of the Bells." It was an interesting song because we incorporated choreography. It was funny because we had to stand on benches and jump off. Trust me there were many times when I was afraid that we would slip and fall. We had our Simply Mystique jackets, pants, boots, and our Santa hats. We did such a good job that Santa asked if we were coming back. We told him we wouldn't mind coming back to sing in front of the crowd again. It was a good promotion for our album and an excellent cause to support the Salvation Army.

The place I remembered the most was near Rockefeller Center where the big Christmas tree was located. We performed on the sidewalk right near that area. The crowd got bigger and bigger each day. We were happy because we helped the Salvation Army while promoting our album. I loved our performances, and it was a great way to continue our dream. We did so many other performances that I can't even keep count.

I remembered we performed for Sparrow at the Labor Day Parade, we sang at the Hilton Head in South Carolina for Amway, and we also did some caroling at the Seaport in N.Y. We did numerous weddings and performed at various churches. I enjoyed the performance with the Salvation Army the most because it was out in the open and it felt like we were giving a concert. There was another performance I remember with Spike Lee. Well, we didn't perform with him, but we were asked to sing the national anthem at a basketball game, and he was there. I heard Spike loved attending basketball games. We were able to meet him and take a picture with him. He was cool! We sang the national anthem, and it was a beautiful experience because we sang it live and acapella. We did it in our style. It was a chance of a lifetime. We performed at Madison Square Garden! We even performed at McDonald's Gospel Fest Semi-Finals, and we performed at the Le Bar Bat club in the city. We had a great experience performing in those places.

God orchestrated our lives. It wasn't meant for us to become famous or superstars, but we were able to live our dreams. We had the chance to do an album, get on talk shows, get on radio stations, and perform in places we didn't think would ever happen to us. We didn't sign a record contract because God was protecting us. I felt that if we were to do one, we had to do it to glorify His name. It wasn't easy to sign with any record label. The way how things are going now in the industry, I'm glad we didn't pursue that route. I knew something was strange when the record labels wanted to change things, but we knew what we wanted, and God had to be in the picture. What the labels were asking for was not in a Godly manner. Record labels were asking us to do things that didn't correspond with our style and views. It clashed with our image of what we wanted Simply Mystique to be portrayed. As I look back on my past experiences with Simply Mystique, I realize that I just wanted to get my foot in the door. I wanted to sing, dance, act and produce. I wanted to do it all. Simply Mystique was a door for singing.

My best friend and I wanted to be hip-hop dancers and we attended so many auditions. The acting came in when I was told by a friend to try to become an extra in films so I could enter the industry. As far as production, I went to college to major in Broadcasting Communications. I would pray every night to God and ask, "Lord, please give me a chance to get my foot in the door to become a performer." My best friend, Selah, and I would attend hip-hop dance auditions and there were so many times that we almost made the audition. I remember there was one audition we wanted to be in and that was LL Cool J's "Mama Said Knock You Out." We didn't make it but the girls who made it look like they were doing some of the moves we did. I couldn't believe it! When Selah told me she was shocked. We didn't make the audition, but they danced like us.

There was another incident when we auditioned, and they called so many names before us that Selah and I decided to leave. When we walked far enough from the audition, someone stopped us and asked, were your names so and so because I think they called your names. I couldn't believe it. We were called finally at an audition, and we walked out before they finished calling the names. We gave up too quickly.

As far as acting, I was an extra on the movie, Royal Tenanbaums with Ben Stiller, Mariah Carey's Glitter, Bad Company with Chris Rock and Anthony Hopkins, Changing Lanes with Ben Affleck and Samuel Jackson, Spider-Man with Tobey Maguire, K-Pax with Jeff Bridges and Kevin Spacey, Anger Management with Adam Sandler and Jack Nicholson, and Bronx Tale with Robert Deniro. I remembered one time I was walking down the street of Manhattan and I saw a trailer. As I passed the trailer, I overheard the person in front of the trailer mention that Denzel Washington is in there. He was filming the Manchurian Candidate. I probably would've seen him if I stayed near the trailer. I was on my way to an appointment so I couldn't stay but it would've been a chance of a lifetime to meet him. I had a great chance to see these wonderful actors in action. I've done theatre and taken acting classes, but it was so long ago. It's 2018 and I just saw the movie Fences starring Denzel Washington and Viola Davis! It was amazing how the movie came out now because I remember that was one of my assignments for my acting class. I played Rose. I've done some real people modeling and again it wasn't huge. It was interesting how God laid my life out for me in the entertainment world. He protected me back then. The only success that got me close to stardom was Simply Mystique. I realized it was because God was the focus of our lives. Everything we did was through prayer and God had to be in the picture. God gave me a taste of what the entertainment business was going to be like but, it was not meant for me to go through this way. God knew my desires and my heart but at the time He knew what was best for me. When I look back, I was trying to figure out what went wrong. God knew what was best for me. He knew what I was able to handle, and He wouldn't give me too much I couldn't bear. I would pray before my dance auditions and acting performances, but God was not being glorified. God gave Simply Mystique a chance to try a bit of the entertainment field, but it was not for us if they were going to change us. We were representing God. We wanted to come out clean, but they wanted to change us a bit. We were not about to change if we didn't do it in God's way. God had to be in the picture. When I look back, I realize that my life would have taken a different turn had it not been for God stepping in and taking over. I was a little concerned because I never thought about anything else but just singing, acting, and dancing. I remember praying and asking God what else I was good at. In college, I chose Acting as my minor and Communications as my major because it was entertainment. Then Simply Mystique broke up. It was my only love that got me close to my dreams. I was sad but it was time to move on. Members were getting married; members were having kids and members had other dreams. For some of them, Simply Mystique was just a hobby. I wanted it to be a career. I prayed and asked God during my sad days what can I do? I wasn't sure if I was good at anything else but entertainment. When I looked back, He had plans but for me to Honor him in a different way. I didn't know what it would be until one day, my miraculous journey with God began. God had to prepare me for doing a mission on his behalf.

CHAPTER 5

THE JOURNEY WITH GOD BEGINS

God has a way of putting people in your life to guide you and to help you. I realized no matter what happened, God was always there. The entertainment field was not horrible as far as working on my talents, but God had a better plan. I moved around a lot when I was a child. During the time with Simply Mystique and auditions, I was living with my family in the North-East. We had a good household and family. Family always sticks together but keep in mind, a family can also have arguments. No family is perfect. I've learned that when I hear stories from other people on their struggles, they've been through as a family I know people went through tougher times than my experience but what I'm about to tell you is about the supernatural. God was showing me how powerful He is and wanted me to work for him.

I wanted to remain in the entertainment business, so I continued to do real people modeling extra work on films, and auditions for dance. I remembered there were so many thoughts going through my head. I wanted to be a backup singer so I can go on tour. I wanted to be a hip-hop dancer for some artists. I figured what could hold me back? I didn't have any children, I was not married, and did not own a house or a car; I was single but lived under my aunt's roof. Yes, under her roof and that was something I had to always remember. There were strange things that started to happen that didn't make any sense. I remember when Selah and I went to visit a hip-hop dance school that took place in the city. We would go a lot to see the choreographers who taught a lot of artists and some that were on tour. It was fun to try a few classes and watch their routines. One day, we went one evening and we noticed the classes were dark. We heard students in there and we thought to ourselves, ok maybe there is a show going on. I've noticed one dancer walking around wearing an outfit that looked like he was going to attend a Zulu tribe ceremony. The Zulu tribe ceremony is the most popular tribe in South Africa. They love to dance and the dancers that we saw had similar outfits. Selah and I walked in and realized there was something a little strange going on. We felt weird! It felt like a wind pushed us back or like a very uncomfortable spirit. I remember that I told her I wanted to go, and she agreed. We quickly went into the elevator to leave the building. She started to speak before me.

She said, "Ingrid, did you feel something weird?"

I said, "Yes, I did! Oh, my goodness! You felt a weird wind feeling too?"

We ran out of the building and looked for a place to sit and talk. We both were like, Ummmmm, I don't think it was meant for us to attend classes this evening. My friend felt it was time to discontinue visiting that place. It was as if God said, "You are not to attend that place." After a while, we wondered if that meant that God didn't want us to pursue dancing anymore. I was also wondering if God didn't want us to continue in the entertainment business. I knew that day God was really protecting us. I started to feel a little sad because I didn't know what else I was good at. I continued to do films as an extra instead. I couldn't make a living doing that because the pay wasn't that high. I guess if you knew you were going to get a check all the time, then it would work. When you're an extra, you get paid by how many days they need you on the set. It was a part-time job for me. I wish it was a full-time job to make a living but that would only work if you're on the set for the whole filming of the movie. I realized I was at a standstill. I couldn't figure out what I was good at that would make me happy. I couldn't find jobs that were stable for me. My best friend and I kept doing temp work and they would not hire for full-time. I used to wonder what was going on. There were a lot of fun, interesting jobs but for some reason, they were not hiring full time. I felt something more and more as I kept praying with God.

I was probably in my twenties when I started to think about people that I wouldn't think of on a regular and I started to have dreams and it would come to pass. I started to think of people and wonder why a certain person is on my mind. Then within minutes, the person would pop up or happen to turn the corner on the street. I would think to myself "No way!" After that, I started to talk to God even more. I started witnessing things that were not normal. I didn't know who to talk to except my closest friend because she could relate. I would have dreams, but I realized that my good friends would have them also. Sometimes when you dream, they may have meanings. It could also mean that God was also talking to you or trying to get your attention. It could mean that it is a warning that something was about to happen. I started to pray with God and started to read the bible. I wanted to build a relationship more with Him because I wanted to understand the strange things that I was experiencing. I started to think about my childhood memories of some supernatural experiences. I started to feel different. There were times that I felt I was not normal like other people. The supernatural stuff started to happen again but mostly at my cousin's house.

Living with my relatives, I started to have dreams that contained a lot of warnings. I started to witness strange things at night. I remember there were a few nights that I wanted to sleep peacefully but in the middle of the night, I couldn't move. My body was stiff, and I couldn't scream or move an inch. It was scary. I started to feel my body lifting out of bed but as soon as I said Jesus in my mind, I felt my body go down and I was able to move again. My heart was pounding, and I got up and read my Bible and I couldn't sleep until the sun came up. I hated that feeling because I felt helpless! It was always during the middle of the night.

There was another strange thing that happened in the house that I couldn't understand. In the middle of one night, I couldn't move, and it happened again. I started to feel something like a stick or a sharp object but keep in mind I couldn't move or open my eyes. It was touching my left foot. I was trying to scream but I could not move. It felt like something was holding me back. After I felt the object lightly touch my left foot, I was able to move again. It felt as if there was something in the room, but I couldn't open my eyes to see what it was. It was a strange feeling. I got up and prayed then continued to sleep because I was dead tired. I then had a dream that my whole left side was darker than my right side. I got up in the morning and started to pray. I was getting scared. I kept asking God what this was all about and asked Him to heal me from that.

There were strange things that happened in that house that I would keep to myself and share only with my close friends who would keep to myself and share only with my close friends who understood me. At times like that, I would wish I could see Jesus and ask him why me? What have I done to deserve this? Who is doing these things to me? I didn't understand. I had no idea what was happening. I wanted to sleep in other rooms, but it didn't make a difference. I would call my friends to pray with me and I didn't feel bad because they would have dreams and experiences also. I remembered watching Benny Hinn on T.V. and saw how he prayed and healed people. I started to read about Jesus and how he healed the blind man, how he raised Lazarus from the dead, and how he healed people on his show through prayer, but I wasn't sure if it was true. One day, something made me watch the show for a few weeks just to see if this was true. One day, he mentioned a woman who was sick. I also knew someone who was sick, and she is a friend of mine, Sarai. I realized that it was true. He mentioned the exact disease and what she had. He asked us to pray for her. I called Sarai and told her what happened. I asked her if she was watching the show and she told me no. I started to pray for her, and she got better. Praise the Lord! She has a wonderful son and he's smart! She's doing a great job raising him. I knew she would be a good mother. I started to read more things about Jesus and wanted to learn more and do God's will.

There was one incident that happened when I was in Junior High School. I remember that we were in the auditorium rehearsing and I was in the chorus. One of the tech teachers told us to sit in our seats. We were not to touch any equipment. I remembered one student touched the mic and started to yell and make jokes and all of us were laughing. The tech guy came out and started to yell at the kid and told him to take his seat. He made an announcement and said if another person goes to the mic, they will get suspended. I don't know what got on my mind that day, but I waited until the tech guy walked away and then I snuck and grabbed the mic and at the same moment, the tech guy came back in.

He yelled, "You! Go to the office, you're suspended! Go get your things and go to the office!"

I couldn't believe I got caught! I was so scared because I knew if one of my relatives found out, I would get into trouble. I started to cry as I went to get my things upstairs in the classroom. I had not been suspended before. I was always a quiet, good girl. I went and got my things then had to take the stairs to go to the office. Suddenly, I took a couple of steps down and slipped and fell. I twisted my ankle. It was a bad day. I got suspended and twisted my ankle and couldn't walk. I limped to the office and the tech guy was waiting to speak to the principal. I walked in limping and told them that I twisted my ankle. The tech guy was telling the principal that I needed to get suspended. The principal told the tech guy to leave, and he'll handle it. The principal told me that I was warned not to be on the mic because I would risk suspension.

The principal then asked, "Why did you go on the mic!"

I said, "I don't know…I felt I had the urge to talk or sing."

The principal said, "You knew that you were going to get suspended and you still went. Well, what's the point of suspending you?" "You just hurt your ankle so what happened?"

I said, "When I went to get my things in the classroom, I slipped down the stairs."

The principal said, "Well, it doesn't make sense to suspend you. You might as well take some days off and heal." The principal didn't call my family since I wasn't suspended. I called for a taxi home. I rested and realized the next day that I couldn't walk. I started crying because I felt like I wasn't going to dance anymore.

I went to the doctor, and he told me, "You may need surgery because you tore a ligament. It can heal but you may not walk the same."

I broke down and cried after I left the office. I started to pray and asked God please I need to heal this knee because I want to continue walking. I was told that I need to go to physical therapy for my knee. It was going to take weeks. I had no insurance and I needed to get this done. I was glad that I had money from my account. I made a savings account from the money my Dad had given to my aunt in the beginning and I would put it into savings. Well, as I told you my Dad stopped coming by to give me some money. I paid the physical therapist and luckily it wasn't expensive. As the weeks rolled by, it was healing but not a hundred percent. I remember the physical therapist was nice and he told me that it will heal but you're not going to be able to dance anymore. You may not jump and do a lot of things as much. I was so devastated. It was as if my goals and dreams were coming to an end.

I went home and cried. I asked God, why? Everything I wanted to do wasn't working. I wanted to make at least $15 per hour and for some reason, I just couldn't receive it from the temp agency. I remember I wanted to continue in the entertainment field, but it just didn't pan out. Things were happening that led to a close. Some things didn't make any sense. One day I walked out of my house, and I didn't limp as much, but my knee wasn't completely healed. I remembered the sun got bright and I looked up at the sky. It was a snowy day. I needed to go for a walk. I cried and said, "God, what will I do?" "What am I going to do next?" I didn't think of anything else to do?" I started to tear up and pray. I said, "God, please, heal me." "I'll do anything you want me to do but please heal me and get me out of here somehow." "If I've done anything wrong, I'm sorry from the bottom of my heart." "What do you want me to do?" Suddenly something strange happened. My knee started to get warm and keep in mind it was snowy that day. I kept praying and said, "In the name of Jesus heal." "God, you can do anything." "Heal me please." My knee started to get this tingling sensation and a warm feeling. I started to feel my knee healing. It felt like a miracle, and I broke down and cried more because I knew God had listened to me. I called my friend and told her what happened. The therapy helped but, it didn't heal my knee completely. The next day, the pain was completely gone, and I started to walk faster and did a little jogging, and it was amazing! I couldn't believe it! I knew from then on God was there watching me. I asked God to continue to guide me and lead me the way He wanted. I continued to temp and then God showed me something else that happened.

There was a temp assignment where I started to work as a receptionist. It was a long-term assignment but of course, it was not full-time. I was working with a nice lady. She was so sweet, but I worried about her because she sometimes came in drunk. I would pray for her and hope that she would heal. I had to help her a couple of times because she was old, and she moved a bit slowly. The stress probably got to her at the job but at the same time, she probably had some other issues. I would talk to her and wanted to keep helping her. I found out she lived alone. One day, she didn't come to work. I received news that she had a brain tumor, so she went to the hospital. I was so sad because I remember she would sometimes come in drunk. I called my best friend and told her that I needed to go to the hospital and see my co-worker. The whole company signed a card and took turns visiting her. My friend met her a couple of times because she would stop by and visit the job. I went and thought about how Jesus healed people. I started to pray and ask God to heal her. I went with my best friend Selah to the hospital, and we brought our Bibles. I started to read some passages that were about Jesus' power of healing. I read about some people that Jesus healed in the Bible before I went. I went to the hospital with my best friend, and I was trying hard not to tear up since she looked brain dead. She had her eyes opened but she couldn't talk or move. She looked like a vegetable. I whispered to her, "Hi, can you hear me?" "It's Ingrid and Selah, remember us?" She didn't move a muscle. She looked as if she was in a coma. No response. I said to Selah, alright let's get to praying. I started to pray and announce how powerful God is and kept giving Him praise. Suddenly, her arm flinched. Selah got a little nervous and I told her to keep praying. We kept going until finally, I felt it was done. She was still like a vegetable, but I told her that we will come back in a few days and pray for her. I figured I will keep going and pray for her at the hospital.

Three days passed and my best friend came back with me to the hospital. We went to the reception and asked if we can see her. We went to her room and found that they were fixing her bed. She wasn't there! My best friend and I went back to the receptionist and asked where she was. They looked her up and said, "Oh, the patient you saw yesterday? Her sister came today and took her. She felt better so her sister came and took her so she can stay with her." My best friend and I mouth dropped. We couldn't believe it! She looked dead as a vegetable. Suddenly, she just felt better like that. My best friend and I just smiled and walked out of the hospital and realized that God really had the power. Jesus was in the house!

I know Selah went and told a couple of people. I did too but I didn't have too many friends. It was a miracle. I started to pray and tell God, wow! I'm speechless! I started to really get into the Bible and read at home. I kept asking God to protect me and be with me.

I started to see God's power more and more around me. I found out years later where my mom was. I spoke to another relative and found out that she was in the town but not too far from where we lived. I haven't connected with her for a while when I found out where she was because I had to mentally prepare myself since I found out that she was sick. It was hard not seeing a parent for years and then finally you hear from a relative that she's in town. I didn't know how to handle it and I didn't know how to react to this issue. I felt a bit upset at myself that I couldn't help her because I was not in a situation to take care of her since I was still living with my aunt. I wanted to go get myself together first before I can do anything. I was still trying to figure out my life. At the time I needed to find out what was my calling or career. It took me a while to go visit my mom a few times and she wasn't fully aware of things because she had a nervous breakdown. I also later found out she had cancer, so I had to go and visit her a few times. It wasn't easy but I finally had the courage to go and see her. I remembered one of my relatives would tell me that I should go and visit her. I told her. I did. It was just that I didn't tell one of my relatives the few times that I went to visit her. I went privately. One relative seemed a bit surprised that I went.

I started to ask God what I should do because I didn't know what I was good at. I started to think about going back to my old college. I told one other relative that I was thinking of going back to school and that relative remained quiet. I thought the person would be a little happy, but the person just had a straight face. I remembered when we won and got picked to go to the Arsenio Hall Show another relative cried. I wasn't sure if it was a cry for happiness or a cry for failure. It felt like that relative probably didn't want me to leave. I wanted to succeed in my dreams but somehow, I felt one of my family members didn't want me to leave. Everyone who lived with us stayed but had a chance to leave. I wanted to leave so badly because I had dreams of traveling and living life. Nothing was working and I couldn't figure out why. Until one day I received an answer from the Lord, God almighty! I witnessed a lot of strange things in my life but this really took the cake.

One day, I was on my way to my best friend's house to hang out. I had walked with my best friend into her building and suddenly we were in the elevator. I turned and asked my best friend how is Ms. Queen doing?

She said, "Ingrid, she's right in front of you."

I said, "Oh, hello."

Now, this was a woman who has a prophetic gift. She had a gift that God would say something and right away she would relay a message to you. I remembered my best friend would tell me about her, but I would question if she was real. I was wondering if she was just a psychic or something. I remember she turned to me in that elevator and started to prophesize, but I also realized it was strange because I had not ever met her before.

She told me, "You need to leave your house. God is going to put you into training. You need to leave because there is something in that house. It's time to go."

What went through my mind was how was I going to leave and where was I going to go. I didn't have enough money to survive.

She said, "When you leave, don't worry about your family. You cannot save your family. When you leave, you to need to leave quietly and wash your clothes before you leave. What one of the relatives did to you was wrong. There was a relative that prayed against you. God is going to put you into training, and you will go from a small place to a big place. Do not worry, God will be with you. I see you will get married but it will be a long time before it happens. It's time to go."

I was in a state of shock because I was wondering how I was going to leave, and I was hurt to find out that it was a family member against me. I bet you this relative was not a horrible person but there were some things that I didn't understand why this person would do them. Anything a relative would ask me to do in the house, I did it. Clean the house, do chores, assist with the hair, assist with feet, assist in cooking. When the woman told me that there was something in the house, I knew what she was talking about because it led me to understand the strange things that happened at night. I started to tear up because when she told me all these things, I was afraid to go home. I couldn't say anything, and I realized it was time for me to leave and do the will of the Lord, but I didn't know how it was going to happen. I walked away with my best friend, and she told me not to worry and keep quiet. I went home and went to my room and slept.

Within that week I connected with another friend, Esther, and told her what happened. Later, Esther decided she was going to leave the state and go to school. Day by day I kept praying and asking God if this is really your message then I will go and do your will. I remember I was at a temp assignment, and I contacted Esther to see how she was doing.

She said, "Have you ever thought about going back to school?" I told her "No, I thought about it, but I didn't know what to major in. I never thought about what I would be good at."

She said, "Fill out the application and just fill out anything. We can become roommates."

I filled out the application and registration forms and remembered what the woman told me. She said, "Leave quietly." Each day I walked into my house thinking how was I going to leave this place? I had dreams of leaving this place. I had dreams of traveling and going into entertainment. It just didn't work out and I couldn't figure out why. When the woman told me that something was in the house and what the relative did to me was wrong. I was really hurt. All my friends who stopped by my house witnessed how I was treated. In Haiti, my friend would say she treated me like a MeMe. In Haiti, a MeMe was considered like a housekeeper or a slave. It was embarrassing because there were times when my friends invited me out, I would tell them I can't because I had to clean the house. My friends would wonder why the other people in the house did not help with the housework. I remember one time I was preparing the chicken and my friend stopped by to help me so I could go out. They all knew and saw it for themselves. Yep! It was a bit embarrassing. I started to pray each day and ask God to take over and tell me how everything was going to happen.

One of my friends called to check on me and asked, "Did you send out the application for the school?" I told her yes. She said OK so check the mail to see if an acceptance letter came. The letter didn't come each time she called and checked. It was soon time for her to go because she received her acceptance letter, but I still didn't. I was thinking about how I told one of my relatives that I wanted to go back to school and wondered if that was a mistake to tell her. Each day I started to pack my things and put them under my bed to hide them. It was a way not to tell anyone in the house. One day I got up and no one was home. The house was bright, and it was sunny that day.

Esther asked, "Did your acceptance letter come in yet?" I told her still not yet.

She said, "Come, don't worry about it, we'll take care of everything when you get here." She asked to please "Stop by my mother's house and she will give you something to give to me."

I remembered I had my Bible, and I was contemplating if I should bring it with me. I looked at it and left it in the middle of my bed. I called my best friend to tell her that I was leaving. I heard her cry and said, "Ingrid go get your blessing!" I left in faith. I called the cab and went to my friend's house. I broke down and cried in front of her mother. I took a few clothes with me, and I remember the woman told me to wash the clothes. Esther's mom was nice, and she told me not to worry and she prayed over me. I didn't take most of the clothes with me, but I was able to leave.

I went to the bus station and all I had was $60. I was worried about how I was going to pay for the bus. I had not checked my balance for a while, and I was uncertain of the amount I had in my account. I didn't know how much money I had in it. I started to pray.

I said, "Ok, God if this is you then what the woman said was true." The man swiped the card and said, "Um…your card doesn't work." The ticket was over $100. I told the man that I only had $60.

He said, "Keep it, here's your ticket."

I was in shock! He gave me a ticket. It was like a free pass. I started to tear up because this was it. My life belonged to God now! It's time to work for the Lord! The bus came to the terminal, and I went to my seat and broke down and cried as the bus moved. It was the beginning of my journey with God. I was leaving to a place where God was going to put me into training. Where did I go? I went to Andrew's University. I basically ran away from home and didn't tell anyone. This was all God's decision. It was time for me to leave and do the will of the Lord. It was time to start my journey with God. This is where my training with God began.

CHAPTER 6

HERE WE GO! IN TRAINING WITH THE LORD!

Here I was, on the bus on my way to a place I have not ever heard of. I was going to Michigan. As I was on the bus, I saw a lot of people. The ride was tiring because it was packed and uncomfortable. It took me until the next day to get to my next destination. Many things went through my mind, but I teared up and realized this is it, my life belongs to the Lord now. I have no idea about this place, Andrews University. I was approaching my destination and my friend Esther told me she would meet me at the bus station. She had a car, and she was there already. We were excited and looking forward to our journey. We went straight to the University.

I met with the Dean of the Girls in the dorm. She was a good friend of Esther's who admired her because she has such confidence in her job… It was ministry. Whenever the ladies had any problems, big or small, she would be there to minister to them. She was awesome! Esther has some awesome friends that she introduced me to. There were some other ladies who also worked at the dorm and were cool. I roomed with Esther. It was small but it was an experience I never had before. I always wanted to know what it would be like to go away for college. I never had the chance to experience that.

Esther had already registered, and I had to soon register. I didn't know what to major in and I had to hurry up and schedule some classes in order to stay in the dorm. I had nowhere else to sleep but in the dorm. It sounds strange to run away to a school, but God had a plan. Within that week, I went to the Registrar's office and registered. I hurried and chose some music classes. I thought maybe I could teach in the future, so I also took an education class. I went to the office, and they asked me if I have been accepted to the school. I told them that I didn't receive my acceptance letter yet, so I just kept waiting and nothing came so I took the risk to just come. I left on faith.

The person got quiet and said, "Well, you came all the way here from another state, no use for you to go back so we might as well schedule your classes."

I couldn't believe it! I told myself, God you got to be kidding! I had the chance to register for school. I realized I didn't even have the money to pay for it. I applied for a loan, and I got it! I got in! I made it into the first semester which was good because that would give me a place to stay and sleep. I went to my room, and I said, "God I really need a hug right now! If you're with me, let me know because I can't believe this happened.

Within a few minutes, one of the RNs of the dorm knocked on my door and said, "Hi, is everything ok?"

She saw me tearing up and she asked, "Would you like a hug?" I really broke down and cried then. It was as if God was listening all that time. He answered my prayers quickly.

She told me, "Ingrid we'll take care of you. You will be ok." I guess she must've heard the story from my friend, and she must've told the Dean. I wouldn't be surprised. There were so many things happening within that week that I didn't know if I was ready to start classes right away, but I had no choice to start. It was time to face reality and move forward and not think about heading back. The first term was ok, but it was hard for me to adjust and focus coming from such a drastic home situation. I've met some wonderful people that my friend introduced me to. I felt like it was too good to be true. I attended a college, but it wasn't anything like this. My friend said, "Welcome to Seventh-Day Adventist University!" "Welcome to Andrews University." It was considered the number one SDA University in the world! I started to meet people from all over the world. It was amazing! I attended a church on campus called Pioneer Memorial Church and found out it was broadcast worldwide with Pastor Dwight Nelson. It was the first church I attended, and I remembered hearing a sermon from Pastor Nelson and I broke down and cried. It was as if God was telling me welcome to your new home.

I attended church and saw some wonderful preachers and students that were becoming preachers. It was a training ground because later I was invited to different ministries. I was Catholic and attending a Seventh Day Adventist University was a great opportunity. I was invited to Sabbath school, and we would have Sabbath lunch. Every Friday, on campus there was always some kind of ministry taking place so my friends would invite me. I had the chance to see how people worship together, pray together and we would have game night. I loved it! I remembered a group called "Journey" and they were good. Esther even invited me to different churches. It was cool! There were so many churches outside of the campus which was awesome because they were unique in their own way. It was also good for the locals, and it was excellent for the students who were in ministry.

I even had a chance to meet some beautiful people in the CELL club. CELL club was another type of ministry. It was a way where they would come in groups and form a cell group. There were so many members that I've met that it's just too many names to name.

We'd laugh together, pray together, like family. I felt like it was a new home. There were so many ministries on campus that I didn't know where to fit in. I wanted to visit as many churches as possible and ministries to see which one grabbed my attention. The church that finally got my attention was New Life Church. I met the wonderful pastor, Timothy Nixon. His wife was very beautiful and friendly. Her name is Sandria Nixon. Tim was the head at the New Life Church located at the seminary. The seminary was a place where all the pastors would train for their degrees. New Life Church was a church located at the seminary. The seminary was a place where all the pastors would train for their degrees. New Life Church was a church that attracted me the most because I can relate to its black culture. They had drums, upbeat music, and the way they praise, and worshiped was exciting. The people were very welcoming. What grabbed my attention the most was the sermon preached by the pastor. I felt when he preaches the word it's inspiring and educational. I really felt the Holy Spirit.

I would meet with the Dean and have Bible study with her. I would have Bible study at other ministries also. I remember Esther told me that I should think about getting baptized. I wasn't sure but I wanted to see more and learn a bit more about being Adventist. It wasn't easy to make a quick decision, so I prayed and continued to visit different ministries. It was soon time to decide, and I decided ok, let me do it because I've noticed that they really stick to the Bible and the Sabbath. I did it! Pastor Timothy Nixon was the one who baptized me. I was proud to have him do it since I saw that he did an excellent job preparing his students for ministry. I had some wonderful prayer warriors and partners. We would get together and pray for each other for everything. I've learned a lot from people, and they made me smile. I loved to see people laugh and look happy. I needed to see that during this time of my life. I even had the chance to visit faculty members' houses on campus. I used to tell myself I'm going to become a pastor. I would visit churches, meet different pastors, watch them preach. I was amazed at some of their preaching.

I remembered applying for the seminary and I didn't get in. I asked the Lord "Why?" "I thought you had wanted me to train?" It wasn't for me. I guess God had another plan and sooner or later God would lead me to it. Now during this time, I was applying to continue to the next term. I had already passed the first term, but I was looking to continue, and I couldn't. Everything came to a halt! I couldn't register for classes because I needed to get a loan in order to continue and I couldn't. I had no one else to really turn to. Esther suggests that maybe it was time to tell my family members where I am because sooner or later, they will call the police and report for a missing person. I prayed and realized the only person I could depend on was Papa. Papa was really my uncle who I lived with in the northeast with my other relatives but he also moved out of the house.

He moved to another state with his daughter. I called and said, "Papa, it's me, Ingrid." He was relieved and happy to hear from me. I finally told him the whole story. I had to let him know that I was safe and that I'm at a university. I'm in school. He had been worried because I ran away but he laughed and said you ran away to a school? It was easy to tell him the name of the school, but I can hear in his voice that no matter what school I was in, he was relieved. I finally had the courage to ask him if I could borrow some money as a loan so I could continue into the next semester. He apologized and told me he didn't have the money. He had already financially helped other members of the family. I told him it was ok. I would figure out a way. I prayed and asked the Lord; it is your will to continue school then ok if not then guide me to move forward somehow.

In the next semester, Esther continued to attend school, but I couldn't, so I had to look for a job. I looked all over campus, and it wasn't easy to find a job right away. It was also time to move into an apartment instead of living in the dorm. Esther found a place not too far from the school. I remembered the woman who had a gift of prophecy and had told me that I was going to move from a small place to a house. She was on point with that. I couldn't believe it! God was really with me every step of the way. Esther found a house that was split into apartments, and we had to pay the rent. Starting out, she was able to pay the rent with the money that she received from her loan in school. I had to hurry up and look for a job. I told myself there was no going back. I kept job-hunting every single day. It wasn't easy especially when I didn't have a car. I asked around and asked friends if they knew of any job openings. I went into stores, schools, clinics etc. There were days that I went to the pond near the house and just prayed. Everything was God and all I had was Him. This was the time when I had to wait on God's timing but man it wasn't easy. There were times that I felt bad and that I was going to be a burden on my friend. I wanted to do extremely well but I couldn't find a job. There were days that I wanted to give up and wonder Lord have you sent me this far to give up????

Days and days went by and still no job. There were days when I felt like I couldn't even talk or face my friend because I felt embarrassed, but she knew it wasn't easy, especially without a car. One day, the phone rang, and I received a call to work at the clinic and it was not too far from the campus. I went to the interview, and I got the job! I jumped for joy. I told Esther that it was a reception job on campus. I felt good because now I could help with the rent. The boss was very nice, and I found out that she had a husband who attended Andrews University also. I also found out that my boss was also new

76

to the job. There were some other new hires, and she was training them. I got hired and a few ladies trained me but there were three receptionists who were mean. They were mean to the new employees. I dreaded going to work every day because they were mean to me also. They were making it difficult for the new employees because they had wanted to get them fired. I guess the new employees were also a threat because the old employees wanted to make sure they keep their jobs. They didn't like the new boss too much so they figured if they could get the new employees fired it would make her look bad. There were many days I teared up and couldn't get myself out of bed because I dreaded going to work. I hated my job, but I was thinking about my friend and the rent. I had to do it and I was thinking to myself there is no going back. I couldn't go back because I knew that God said He would take care of me. Each day, those three ladies made my life a living hell and one by one the new employees quit. Each time they yelled at me I kept messing up. They would do it on purpose. I was practically the last person left and the boss was trying to hire more people. It was coming to a point where I wasn't sure if I could make it anymore.

I remember I started to just let the phones ring off the hook and the ladies started laughing. I took one call, and it was a doctor. Our job was to page the doctor if another doctor calls. I didn't page the doctor. I gave up and told myself, I'll just get fired. One of the ladies found out and ran back and said, "We got her! We got her!" They were giggling and saying, "She's going to get fired." Suddenly, my boss called and said, "Ingrid, come to my office." The ladies in the background started to laugh. My boss told me to close the door and have a seat.

She said, "Ingrid, did you receive a call from the doctor?"

I said, "Yes."

She said, "Were you not supposed to page the doctor?"

I said, "Yes."

She said, "You know this right?" "Why didn't you page the doctor?"

I started to tear up a bit and I shrugged my shoulders like I did not know or care.

She said, "You know Ingrid something like this can get you fired."

I just teared up and said, "Oh well."

At that moment what went through my head was that it was over. It was time to get fired.

She said, "Ingrid, go outside and take a break and get some air." I looked at her in shock. I was thinking to myself what just happened? She was supposed to fire me. I went down the hallway and noticed how everyone was laughing at me and felt that they succeeded because they wanted me fired and were trying to make the boss look bad. I went outside for a walk and then I saw a bench. I sat there and broke down and cried. I said, "God, I don't understand!" "This is too hard!" "I don't know if I'm good at anything." Then suddenly, I remembered the sun got brighter and I had a warm feeling. The sun was beaming brightly on my face. The Lord spoke to me.

God said, "You forgot where you came from." "You need to know who you are." "Do you think I sent you all the way out here for nothing?" "Now, get back in there and you will know who you are."

It was a weird feeling because there was no one around and it was like no wind was blowing at all. Just silence. I wiped my face and stood tall and marched back into the office. As I walked back in, everyone was quiet and continued their work. I slowly walked to my desk and slowly began to pick up the phones.

My boss came up to me and said, "Are you ok?"

I said, "Yes."

She said, "Come into my office."

Once I stepped into her office she said, "Ingrid, I decided that you are going to help me change this whole place around."

I said, "Me?" "What do you mean?"

She said, "You'll be my assistant. We'll continue to talk later."

She said, "You can go back to your desk."

I went back to my desk and smiled. I thought about what God told me and I teared up a bit with joy.

The three mean ladies started coming to work late and so the boss would ask me to help her and cover their spots. There were days that these ladies didn't even come into work so I had to cover for all of them. It would not make the boss look bad and, in the meantime, she was interviewing other workers. The three ladies kept coming in late or not coming in and I had to cover for them at the same time the new workers would come in and my boss asked me to train them. I couldn't believe that I would be the one training them, but I did it. Little by little, we had a full staff of new people. One day the boss went to the doctors and said, "You know you should think about firing these three ladies." The doctors felt that these three ladies had been there for years. The boss mentioned that the ladies were always late or absent and that I covered for them. She mentioned that she had to hire new employees because they didn't come in often enough and I had to ask Ingrid to train the new employees. She questioned them about the quality of employees they wanted working in their office. The doctors got quiet then said, "It would make sense to hire Ingrid.

One by one, the three ladies got fired and we had new staff. I couldn't believe it. My boss put me in charge of training the new hires at the job. I still couldn't believe it! I was training new people! I kept remembering God when He spoke to me and reminded me of who I am. Little by little things, got better at the job and people were friendly and we had parties etc.... The whole place changed for the better. I looked forward to coming to work.

It was soon time for my boss to leave as her husband was graduating from Andrews University. She suggested that I look for another job because things were not working out well in the new position for me. I used my paycheck to buy a bike. I didn't care because I got myself into shape. It felt like every time someone would say something bad about me or make fun of me, God would turn it around for the good.

I later went for another job and had to move someplace else. I met another good friend at the job, and she asked if I wanted to be her roommate. God opened another door because it was time to move out of the house, I was in. This time, the job was a little better and the people were a bit nicer. I was able to meet another Adventist at the job. Her name was Vashti. I was able to attend her church and meet some more Adventist people. I later met another nice friend who also opened her home to me if I needed a place to stay and her name is Mel. I thank God that He used these people in my life. It was amazing how God used them to help other people. They are still blessed today.

I remember on campus there were a lot of nice men. Many of the women wanted that same man. I'll never forget that one of my cousins said to me, no matter how many women you throw in front of one man, the man gets to choose. It's not easy but with my luck every time there was someone I liked, another girl would like the guy and I didn't get him. I remember there was this pastor who all the ladies had a crush on. They all wanted to be with him. He was handsome and very intelligent. I remember I would stop by and see him preach and sometimes see him at different ministries. I would say hi to him, but I realized that some of the women had a better chance because they hung out with him and they know him very well. I always felt like I was not good enough. I would look at the other ladies and they had cars, looked prettier, dressed better etc... And what did I have? A bike and hand me down clothes. Of course, I appreciated the clothes that I had, and I didn't care because I was so happy that someone nice had given them to me. There were some women who would laugh because of it. I didn't care as long as I get to work and paid the bills. I later noticed that little by little the ladies started to work out a lot. As I went to church, I met a lot of guys, and they were friendly to me. I guess riding the bike to work paid off after all because I got into shape. More and more the popular guy kept saying hi to me more and we would chat as friends. It gave me a chance to see what type of guy he was.

I later found out he dated one of the Deans. I was happy because she was nice, and I've seen how friendly they got along. Some people thought that I was trying to get him badly, but I was just friends with him. I made him cheesecake, just as a courtesy. Later, the Dean broke up with him and I still didn't have a chance. I guess I was not his type but when I look back now, I realized he was better with the woman he's with now. They look perfect together. I started to learn that it's not worth it to force yourself towards any guy. When God sends you that right man, you wouldn't have to fight for it. What's yours is yours.

The University was an excellent experience for me. I learned a lot. There was one other ministry that grabbed my attention, and it was called FUSION. FUSION took place every Friday night on the sabbath, and it was a place where people would come together and worship with song. I heard it started when a lady by the name of Mary was on campus and noticed that there were a lot of ministries, but they were not mingling among each other. It was like all the groups kept to themselves. There was no love and no togetherness. She wanted to try to have a song of worship to bring people altogether. Esther was able to start and lead the worship service. It began to be popular. It was like attending a concert, but it was beautiful because people were able to pray together and worship with song. I always looked forward to being there. Esther was the person I would watch and learn from in order to fit in with the Adventist crowd since she was Adventist.

I used to walk around the concert hall and pray before the concert would start. I would sit up front and give Esther support. She helped me so much so the least that I could do was to give her support. FUSION had gotten so popular that it spread throughout other Adventist Universities. It was a success! It kept going and it was good to see the students getting involved. We had a lot of good leaders on campus. Attending FUSION was like attending a concert. When I think about concerts, I was thinking back in the past about how I wanted to audition to go on tour. Keep in mind that I didn't tell too many people about my experience in the entertainment industry. I knew my life was for God and He would lead me to where He wanted me to go. I performed on FUSION before but I wasn't a student so I would still visit the campus to find out which ministry was good.

One day, I've met another friend who was also involved in a ministry on campus. She was so sweet. She married a good guy later and they are fantastic together. She bumped into me one day and she told me her experience as a Missionary. I asked her what it was like. She told me that it involved teaching English and Bible studies. She said to me that I would love it. It worked out because it was time for my roommate to move and I had to find a new place. I researched and met the representative for the Mission, which took place in South Korea. I was so scared because I had never left the country by myself before. It was tough but I had to do it. There was no going back. I went by myself to get my passport and visa. I saved some money, and it was time to figure it out on my own. I realized it wasn't meant for me to continue school since I didn't have the money and it wasn't meant for me to go into the Seminary. I spoke to my pastor about it, and he said maybe it's meant for you to become a Missionary. I went around and gave my last goodbyes to my friends and prepared for my next journey. It was a way for me to make money and for me to do the will of the Lord. It was a journey far away from home, but I was working for the Lord. I kept reminding myself that my life belongs to God now.

CHAPTER 7

OK, GOD! LET'S DO THIS! MY MISSION IN SOUTH KOREA!

I was on my way to the airport. I was excited but at the same time, I was scared because I have never been far away from home alone in another country. My friends were telling me not to worry because you won't be alone, and you'll meet other missionaries there. I remembered my friend who had been in South Korea told me that I was going to have a blast. I kept thinking to myself maybe they are only going to have tents to sleep in, but I found a big, major city. It was my first time flying for so long on a plane. It was about 14 hours away! I had to walk around the plane a couple of times because for me to sit still all those hours made my body numb. When it was finally time to land, I realized that there were not too many black people on the plane. Everyone was Korean. I thought to myself that they were going to realize that I'm a foreigner. I got off the plane and went through customs, immigration, and baggage claim with no problems. I was told to look for someone with a sign SDA Samyook. All of a sudden, I see a tall blonde-haired man standing there with glasses. He looked serious and at the same time, I wondered if he was going to be mean. Strangely enough, he was friendly.

He said, "Hi, Are you, Ingrid?"

I said, "Yes."

He said, "Hi, my name is Mr. Arthur, and I will take you to where you're staying."

I was relieved because I really wanted to be around nice people. I remembered we stopped quickly to grab something to eat then we made it to our destination. The place looked like an alleyway; it was a small place, and I met some other teachers there also. Mr. Arthur let me know that this was the place where I was going to stay and reminded us about tomorrow. He brought in the luggage and left. I met most of the teachers from South Africa in my dorm. I don't remember their names, but they were friendly, and they made me feel comfortable. I was told the next day was orientation and I would meet a lot of other teachers. I felt like I was back at my dorm at Andrews University. We were up laughing, joking around and it was soon getting late into the morning. We finally got some shuteye to prepare for the next day.

It was morning and it was time for us to get up. We ironed our clothes, took showers, and cooked breakfast. I realized we were not too far from the place we had to go. They had a nice buffet set up for us so we could have breakfast. We met some wonderful people, and they came from all over. We met people from Africa, North America, South America, Europe, Asia, and Australia. I was amazed because it gave me an opportunity to meet people from around the world. It was nice because we had a song service. We sang songs from hymnals and sang other worship songs. We met some people who oversaw the administration during the time I was there. They were very pleasant and helpful. Each of them gave a speech about what was expected in our Mission.

I knew our goal was to spread the word of Jesus all across the world, but I didn't understand how teaching English was considered a mission. We were told we were expected to do Bible Studies with our Korean students. Every Friday, we were required to lead a song service and give a presentation like a sermon. I was nervous because

I had never done a PowerPoint presentation before. What I loved most about the teachers was that we worked together as a team, and we were able to learn from each other. We were also required to attend church every Saturday. At orientation, they showed us how this became a mission. They showed us step by step how to teach English. We were to give the Korean students words and have them pronounce them several times. We had a time limit then we would do some grammar. We also had a time limit and then the rest of the class was for conversation. It became a routine. The students were also required to do a certain amount of listening time. The book was used by the Samyook Language School, and it was organized and set up for each day. The book had day one, day two, day three, etc… Each day, there was also a Bible verse on the board then we would explain it to the students before we started our lesson. We would also pray before we begin our lesson. It was nice. I remembered one teacher asked how this is a mission for them to learn about Jesus. I've noticed the Bible verse written each day on the board would introduce them to what we read in the Bible, but I was also curious to know how else we can lead them to learn about Jesus? They taught us at orientation that we will also be doing Bible studies outside of class hours and do a sermon on Fridays. We were to invite the students to come to church also. I finally figured it out! When we invited the students to Bible study, this was a way for them to learn more English and to learn about the Bible. It was also a time to get to know the students more. Friday night was worship service so we would give them a presentation and they would do some reading and singing. It was brilliant! After orientation, it was time for all the teachers to be sent to their different schools.

Seoul was the main place where all the schools would meet up for orientation and it was also a place where they had church. I don't remember the first school I was sent to but I do remember my last school was Cheonan and before was Suncheon. We were sent to our schools and to our accommodations. It was cool because I had the chance to room with other teachers. The school was going to start right away within the same week. I think there were three roommates but there was always a Korean teacher. The Korean teachers were nice. I realized that Koreans are very nice people. I had a chance to taste Korean food. There were different types of dishes but what I loved the most was that it looked healthy and it wasn't greasy or fattening. The Korean teachers would make dishes and have us taste them. They were good. They had Bibimbap which had vegetables and rice, Bulgogi and Gimbop, which was my favorite because it was just seaweed wrapped with rice and vegetables. Kimchi is a popular dish in Korea that they eat very hot sometimes. It's just raw cabbage. Miyeok-gul and Haejang-guk are different types of soups. Jajan myeon is a special sauce with vegetables and rice. There were more dishes that I know I must've tasted but I don't remember all their names. It wasn't easy to pronounce some of their names, but they were delicious.

The school was starting and it was the first day of class and I was nervous but I had to get over my fear of speaking in front of the classroom. I remember I wrote down what I had to say before I forgot some things but strangely enough, the students made me feel very comfortable. I did the mapped-out lesson as planned but I was really nervous. I felt good because I was by myself in the classroom. If I had someone watching me or monitoring me, it would have made me even more nervous. When I get nervous, I mess up badly. I tend to be a klutz. I was shaking but I made it through my first class. The students were very attentive, and they were willing to learn. I have really appreciated it. The best part of the class was conversation time because it gave the students enough time to communicate with each other. I made them introduce themselves and communicate with each other. It was beautiful. I even told them what was required to pass, and they actually did it.

The students in South Korea are very intelligent. They're also very hard on themselves. I would tell them that they are beautiful, and they are doing extremely well in class but some would think their speech was not that good or their pronunciation was not clear. I would tell them it's ok, if you ever visited the United States, everyone would understand what you were saying, even if you had an accent. Some would think that they wanted to learn English and sound like me right away. In South Korea, their mentality is to get things done quickly. You will notice everything is fast-paced. You will not see any lines and if you do, they will yell to make you go faster. The students believe in education, and they are very driven. If the students don't pass, they feel like their world is over. When they practice culturally, the students would give gifts to the teachers, and I remember the first time a student gave me a gift.

I said, "It's ok, you don't have to give me a gift."

The student sat in the back and didn't participate that much during conversation time. If I called on the student, the student was reluctant to answer.

One day, one of the other students who were his friend said, "Teacher, he gave you a gift because he appreciated you."

I told her, "It was ok. He didn't have to give it to me."

She explained to me that in Korean culture, a teacher is considered a master. They are to be always respected. When a student gives a gift to a teacher, the teacher must accept it as a token of appreciation. It is their culture. I felt so guilty and embarrassed I didn't know what to say. I took the gift the wrong way. I thought that he was a male student who had given me a gift to pass the class. I felt so bad. I continued the conversation and wanted to learn more about their culture. I wanted to get advice on how to make up for not accepting the gift. She suggested that I bring a gift too. I told her is it ok if I bring in chocolates for the class and I'll give him special chocolate?"

She said, "Sure."

The next day, I brought in chocolates and gave them to them during conversation time. I went to the student and gave him an individual box of chocolates by Godiva while the whole class had Dove chocolates. I gave him a box and I said, "I'm sorry that I didn't accept your gift." "Would you please accept mine as an apology for I didn't understand the reason why you gave me a gift?" "I took it the wrong way and I'm sorry." "I'm interested to learn more about your culture."

He smiled and said, "Oh, yes teacher!" "We can show you around Korea one day if you have free time outside of class."

I said, "Sure, why not?"

He looked excited, accepted the gift, and said thank you, teacher. The students all smiled and were looking forward to attending class more and more.

I was told that at the end of the semester the students can have parties. I was so happy to hear that. It gave me a chance to get to know the students more and we practiced more English. I also noticed that the students were allowed to take the teachers out for lunch. One of the students even took me to karaoke. They took me to many places and so many restaurants which I felt was a smart move because it still gave them a chance to learn English. I told them to watch English TV shows, buy English books and make some foreign friends so they can practice speaking with them. My big adjustment was the time difference because we were on the other side of the planet. I also invited some students to Bible study, and I now understood how the mission came into play.

In South Korea, their culture was interesting. They are very friendly people but there are some things that make them unfriendly, like pushing and not saying excuse me. I was going to push the person back but luckily a student was next to me, and she told me that it's normal here in this country. Everything is fast-paced and if they must get somewhere and you're in their way, they just move you aside but not harshly but in a manner for them to carefully get to their destination. I also learned that they're sensitive to certain matters. Because they're very hard on themselves in their culture, if they don't succeed, they feel as if they failed. Some, when they fail, take their lives. I was shocked to find out they commit suicide very often. I've met many students in Bible study, and some would speak to me privately about their personal problems. I've realized there were a few students that were alcoholics. We are not allowed any alcohol in our language institutes. We have a lot of SDA language institutes in South Korea, and we had to set a standard for our beliefs. The students would drink and sometimes look drunk. I remember seeing a young lady in the street laid out and her guy friend came out and picked her up and brought her home. I noticed that there was a club and she laid not too far from the door. You would see people walk drunk sometimes. During our Bible study, I would ask the students why some students drink a lot. Some students told me that they feel pressure from home. The pressure sometimes comes from their parents because they push them very hard. If they fail, it would be considered a loss of face. In order to deal with the lack of embarrassment sometimes, they would kill themselves. It was a way to not deal with the shame. Shame in their culture was not good for them.

Our mission was to explain that it is okay to continue to live. Many of the students were not religious and they didn't know about Jesus. This is where I felt our mission came in. In Bible study, we were able to teach them English, but it was also a way to introduce them to Jesus. We had a chance to explain who Jesus was and what Jesus taught us and the importance of our existence. I had to explain that Jesus taught us not to take our own life because God is the one to judge, not us. It was a way to let them know that killing yourself is not a Godly act. It is a copout. It was a way to let them know that they had potential but I encouraged them and taught them to believe in themselves. My motto was "You Can Do It!" I always said that to encourage them during an exam. I loved when they repeated the motto and said, "Yes, teacher I can do it!" The students were diligent, so I didn't have to worry about their work. Throughout the term, they were able to do the work but what I enjoyed the most was how they improved. There were times that I felt sad if I saw the students coming in with red eyes. I knew they went drinking the night before.

There were many times I had to invite the students to Bible study and to Friday Night's Vespers because I wanted to share with them that killing yourself is not a good thing. There are many things to do in this life and committing suicide is not the answer. If it wasn't for God to be in my life, I wouldn't know what to do. I would enjoy it when some of the students would hear my testimonies and they would become more interested. I noticed more students would come.

I've met so many wonderful students and again they were too many to name. Some of the students were very challenging and would ask so many questions about the Bible that I didn't have an answer to. I would say, "I'll get back to you with that answer tomorrow." I had a wonderful time with the students because they were willing to try, and they did not give me a hard time. There were some students I would worry about, and I would speak to them privately after class but, most of the students enjoyed inviting me to some places.

I visited so many places in South Korea. The students took me everywhere. They would invite me to the cinema. They would take me to the mountains. They would invite me to the music fountain. The music fountain is popular in South Korea because there were different colored lights with the fountain bouncing up and down to the beat of the music. I enjoyed their parks. The institute would take us to picnics. I joined their gyms. I loved their outdoor concerts. They sang Korean most of the time, but I loved some of their arrangements. Some of the students would tell me about their favorite artists and they would show me their videos. At the time I was there I liked 2NE1, a girl group, Girls' Generation, and the boy band, Big Bang. There were two male artists that I remembered which were PSY and Rain. PSY did the song "Gangnam Style" which became popular in the U.S. Rain had a cool song called, "Rainism." They had wonderful spas and their technology was advanced. I remembered that when I had to go to the dentist and had seen their incredible equipment! The spas were not easy for me to adjust to because you had to be naked. They had hot saunas, but I didn't realize we couldn't go in with our bathing suits. It took me a while to open and get naked in front of other women because it was really embarrassing. I remember the first time I went; I brought my bathing suit and they insisted that I could not wear it because they did not wear theirs. Well, I walked out! It wasn't easy for me to do that, but it had to take a few teachers to come with me to get the courage. The teachers would tell me that it's ok, for goodness' sake we all have the same private parts I was going through a body shame phase. I felt so uncomfortable at first that I stayed underwater for quite some time so I wouldn't have to get out. When I wanted to go to the next pool, I would rush out quickly and jump into another pool and stay underwater for a while. Yeah, it took me a while to get comfortable. I'm still a virgin and I had never been naked in front of other women and not a man.

There were other places that I would visit like Gyeongbokgung with its historic palace that had tours and museums. N Seoul Tower had a city view and restaurants. Everland had amusement parks with rides and zoo animals. I went to Busan, Jeju City, Incheon, Gyeongju, and tons of other places that I know I'm not going to remember now but they were all beautiful. There was definitely an area for foreigners, and they would have their shops and sell foreign goods. I was happy to see black hair shops where they sold black hair products. It was so easy to get around in South Korea because you didn't need a car. It's like a hop skip and a jump to get to other destinations. I was able to go from city to city with no problems. I loved traveling. We would teach for a year and go home for the summer. On our breaks, we would have the luxury to travel to other countries. I loved it. I was able to travel to China, Japan, and Israel during my breaks. I was living my dream and it was one of the best things that had ever happened to me.

I stayed in South Korea for three years but then there was word that they were going to shut a few of the institutes down. I think they were losing money. On one of my teaching days, I started to pray, and God told me to meet him in Israel. I figured ok well it's going to be break time for us, so it was a perfect time to book a flight. I don't remember the holiday in Korea, but it was enough time for us to come back and continue the rest of the school year. I thought I was hearing things, but I prayed and said if this is you, Lord then you will make a way for me to go. I looked at my savings and it was just enough for me to book a ticket. God was showing me that He was guiding me.

Israel

I booked my flight to Israel. It was a pleasant flight, but I wanted to test if God is still around me. I got on the plane and sat in my seat. I took out my pocket Bible and started to pray before takeoff. I closed my eyes and whispered, "God if you are here with me let someone come right in front of me." Within minutes a Jewish man came right in front and started to pray against the wall. My eyes got wide, and I said to myself maybe that's just a coincidence. I said it again, "God if you're with me then let another man come in front of me." Within minutes another guy came and prayed against the wall in front of me on the plane. I said to myself, "No way." I started to shake a bit because that made me a bit nervous, and I started to really get into the chapter in the Bible. They started to turn off the lights on the plane. I started to close my eyes God told me, "Now, you know it is me. Meet me in Israel." I was calm but a bit nervous about what God had in store for me. It was a pleasant flight, and it was soon time to land. We got off the plane and I started to look for my tour group. I went with the tour group to our hotel, and it was beautiful.

The next day we started our tour. We went to Gethsemane where Jesus was, and we saw the place where Jesus died on the cross. They built a church around the area. We even went to the river Jordan. We had the chance to touch the tomb where Jesus had laid. I started to get emotional because of the thought of what Jesus had to do to save us. What a sacrifice! God loved us so much that He gave His only son. One place that grabbed my attention was the Wailing Wall. I've noticed some people wrote their prayers on a piece of paper and put it on the wall then they started to walk backward. I asked the tour guide why they were walking backwards? He told us they were walking backward because you are not to turn your back on God. I thought to myself that was awesome! The Wall was split with one side for the women and one side for the men. I figured let me go and try so I wrote my prayer requests and put them against the wall. I walked backward and sat at the bench in the back.

What I'm about to tell you next may be a bit strange. One of the people in my tour group was at the Wailing Wall. I was in the middle of prayer on the bench in the back. He looked like he was looking for someone but all I did was look up quickly because I was in prayer. I noticed there was a split of people between me and him. He looked dead at me, and I was wondering if he was going to walk towards me and he didn't. He couldn't miss me because I was in the open. I guess he wasn't looking for me. I turned my head and returned to my prayer. After I prayed, I went to our meeting spot. I met the members.

The man who I saw at the Wailing Wall said, "Where were you? I was looking for you." I looked at him like he was crazy.

I said, "I saw you looking dead at me on the bench. Why didn't you come to me?"

He said, "What are you talking about, I didn't see you at all." I got quiet and was looking at him like he was nuts.

I said, "I was there. I saw you clearly. I was all the way at the back on the benches."

He said, "That's impossible!"

I said, "Why would you say that?"

He said, "Because I looked back where the benches were and there was no one there." I got quiet and the tour guide told us it was ok because everyone was there and we could go on with the rest of the tour.

I turned to the guy and pulled him aside quietly, asking, "Are you serious?" "You really didn't see me?" I saw you looking dead at me, and you were not too far from me."

He said, "Ma'am, I'm serious, I didn't see anyone at the bench." I remained quiet for the remainder of the trip because that was strange. When the tour was over, we were all sent to our hotels. I later went to my room and prayed. God told me to meet him tomorrow.

The next day, we went near some parks and of course, we had a meeting point. I went towards some other benches near the sea. It was beautiful. I started to close my eyes and enjoy the calm sun. All of a sudden, I heard God saying, "Ingrid, this will be your last year in South Korea. You will go home and spend some time with the family. You will not stay long. You will leave the U.S. again. I will send you to the Middle East next." I looked around me and noticed there was no one around me. I started to walk back slowly and wondered how this was going to happen. I went back to my hotel room, and it was soon time to end our tour.

I went back to South Korea from my trip since it was during our break. The administration called for all the teachers to come together for an important meeting. I got worried and wondered what the meeting could be about. All the teachers from different institutes met up and waited for the administration to arrive. The president of the Institute showed up as well. The announcement was that they were shutting down another institute. They even mentioned shutting down some more because of the lack of money. In order for this mission to continue, they will have to try not to make the institute only SDA. They would have to mix it into a government issue probably because we need government funding. It will no longer be a Seventh Day Adventist institution it will be a public institution. We still teach English but would have to change the program in a way to cater to all people. I'm not sure if there were going to be prayer times or the mission will discontinue. I just heard that church will be available, but I wasn't sure if we would be able to evangelize as much. My mouth dropped! I was in a state of shock because I was just in Israel and God told me this would be my last year. I understand the reason now. It was time to move. I guess I was going to the Middle East but where?

CHAPTER 8

TO THE MIDDLE EAST, YOU GO THUS SAYS THE LORD!

I knew what God told me was true, but I didn't know it was going to happen so fast and I was excited because the first place I thought about was Dubai. I thought to myself that maybe God will send me to Dubai. Dubai was considered the talk of the town. I looked online at the country and it's amazing! I continued praying and told the Lord, I'll go where you'll send me. I just didn't know how it was going to happen, but I guessed I would find out when I head home. I remember the Lord told me that I was going to spend time with my family and friends.

It was time for all the missionaries to head home and continue with their lives. Some stayed a bit longer in South Korea but most left. I got on the plane and headed home to spend some time with the family. I contacted other family members that lived in the Southeast. I had asked if it was ok to stay with them and they had no problem with the situation. They understood and found out that it was time to leave the Northeast. I didn't go back to the Northeast. I stayed with my other family in the Southeast. While I was staying with my family in the Southeast, the family from the Northeast came to visit. We had a wonderful time, and it gave us a chance to resolve our issues. We sat and communicated to solve some issues. They understood that it was time for me to continue to move on and live. The family from the Northeast understood that there was no coming back to live with them, but I have no choice to come back and visit anytime. They just wanted to make sure that I get myself together. It was time for the family from the Northeast to head back home because they only stayed for the weekend to visit. We all hugged each other and continued traveling back. It felt good to finally catch up and communicate through phone, internet, etc… when we got the chance. While I was staying with my family in the Southeast, I had to think about creating an income while I was staying there to help them out, so I decided to go online and look for any job since I knew I was only going to stay temporarily. Papa was so pleased to see me home, so we hung out a lot. I would take him driving to different places. It was a lot of fun, and he had such wisdom. I used to always look forward to hearing his stories, especially his experience in World War II. I couldn't believe it! He was in World War II! He used to tell me incredible stories about Harlem. He even told me how they used to wear zoot suits back then… There were other styles in his days, but it was awesome to hear about them and realize what he lived through. The best part was that he was alive to see an African American President of the United States! It was a long way coming. He lived to see President Obama!

My family from the Southeast loved to give parties and celebrate holiday events. We were known for our cool cookouts and block parties. Our family was the talk of the town. I started job searching and I took anything. One relative told me about working in Target. I just told her no problem and that I would take any job for now. As a Missionary, I enjoyed teaching English, so I wanted to continue to do this as an ex-pat. I did my research and I remember a friend of mine from church mentioned that I needed to get a CELTA certificate because it was globally recognized. All jobs overseas accepted the CELTA and so I did my research, and I found a school that I could attend to take it.

Where was the school? It was in the Northeast. I was staying with other family members in another town of Northwest. It was convenient for me. I didn't want to stay in the northeast since God told me I had to leave there. I decided to contact another relative and ask if I could stay with him and he welcomed me with no problem. He was awesome because he had a great company, he was running a company called ON2. It was amazing because every year he would throw an event at a hotel with his other friends, and they would promote salsa classes. It was amazing how his company got started. He was brilliant. He started taking salsa classes in his town and he noticed they had T-shirts. I guess the dancers always had T-shirts on. He figured he would get some T-shirts made and sell them. He started to sell them, and he became popular with them. He started to come up with other ideas to make caps, different types of T-shirts etc…He then started a website and started selling his products and sell. His business got bigger and more popular. He would collaborate with other employees to promote the school, his products, and other people's products at an event every year. Well, it was amazing to finally visit his annual event. I stayed with him a bit so I could attend the CELTA school in New York.

I told him not to tell too many people that I was working on my CELTA certificate because some people may not understand. I learned sometimes you can't tell big dreams to small-minded people. I learned that from watching Steve Harvey. I remember I told Papa about going to school for the CELTA and he would push me and say I was going to make it. I had another relative who was a teacher so she would assist me while I was taking the classes.

It was the first day of the CELTA class and I wasn't too happy because I had to attend classes on the weekend. It was supposed to be a day of rest for me. They had another alternative to working straight hours for five days, not including the weekends but you had to be picked for that. I've met some wonderful students and it was awesome because there were students from different countries. I got excited because it gave me a chance to think about traveling overseas. The course was difficult. I didn't think I was going to make it because there was a lot to do in a small length of time. My family members kept pushing me and I had help from the relative who was a teacher. She aided me the most along the way. I will always thank her for that. When it got towards the end of the course, I crashed. We had one more assignment and then I broke down and cried. I didn't think that I could do it. It was overwhelming and thoughts went through my head thinking that I was not good enough for this. As I broke down and cried, my teacher came and helped me. It was my last assignment, and I don't know why I crashed. I was a little embarrassed, but he helped me because he knew I would be ok as a teacher. After crying, I decided to shake myself up and say to myself, "Come on Ingrid!" "You didn't get this far for nothing!" Each student was put in a group and each of us had to conduct a lesson. We all make it and passed! We were all excited. I'm a big advocate for teamwork. I always love to see people work together as a team. When people work together as a team, things get done faster, different ideas are shared, and the group will succeed quickly together. We all received our certificate, and it was time to start choosing our location to work overseas. I remember I met a teacher from India and Pakistan. They told me about the Middle East. I was afraid because I heard bad stories about the countries over there. They would tell me not to worry, it's safe. They encouraged me to research for myself rather than just believe the news because they exaggerated a lot. As soon as they told me about the Middle East, I suddenly thought about what God told me.

That's it! This is how I will go to the Middle East!

I started to go online and check some websites for jobs. My mind was on Dubai, so I kept applying for it. I was told by a friend to check out other places like Saudi Arabia, Kuwait, and Bahrain. I was a little scared to try those countries because of the news but I did my research and asked around. I kept thinking about the teachers in my CELTA class when they told me that it was not that bad. I clicked for the other countries and for some reason Saudi Arabia kept popping up. I didn't know anything about that country, so I did my research and spoke to someone about it. I wasn't too adamant about it because I heard the women had to cover themselves. I didn't hear about that for Dubai. I found out that in Saudi Arabia, men and women are not allowed to mingle together. The women are not allowed to drive. The more I was noticed how limited the women were in that country I started to feel discouraged. I wasn't too happy, but I kept praying and asking God if this was for real. I found out Saudi Arabia as an Islamic nation. I thought to myself, how was I going to spread the word about Jesus in this country? I could easily get into trouble! I heard you could get put into jail for certain things. I kept applying for Dubai and Saudi Arabia kept popping up. Within a few days, I received a call for an interview for Saudi Arabia. I did the interview and passed. I was excited! I was also connected with someone who had the experience of working in the Middle East and she was from the United States... she told me it was fine. She told me that the women would be in accommodation together and have their own bus, so the company will make sure the women are safe. My family was excited so I was ready to do God's will. I had no idea where God was going with this, but I realized that God always has a plan. When God says go, you must go! It was time! I got my documents together and went to the Saudi embassy to pick up the visa. I went to get my plane ticket and was told that I would be reimbursed for it. I was off to the airport with the family, and they gave their goodbyes. I was nervous because I had to prepare myself mentally for entering a country that had certain rules that were different than our country America. I quickly went to my seat and looked at the map to see how many hours it will take to get there. I noticed it will take about 17 hours. Whew! I later knew it was time to relax and prepare for a long ride. During the plane ride, they had films that you can watch so that was a great way to kill time. I landed and I noticed how beautiful the airport looked because there was a fountain. I saw most of the men had their thobes on. In Saudi Arabia, I researched and found that the thobes were traditional clothing from thousands of years and their ancestors wore it and wore it as an identity to show that they are proud of their roots. It was made suitable for the environment as the roomy clothes help keep you cool and more comfortable. I felt a little better because I saw some women who were from the United States and the UK online. I went online there so someone can greet me. I was a little concerned because I was expecting someone to come and pick me up at the airport in Saudi Arabia to give me a ride to my accommodation. I guess it wasn't like South Korea. I decided to make a call. Of course, with my luck, I couldn't make a phone call on my phone since I was in another country. I decided to speak to someone behind the counter for a traveling agency. He was Indian. He was nice enough to let me use his phone to make a phone call. I'm glad because I had in my mind that women are not to get close with the men there. I called and finally, someone picked up and he was the administrator in the office. He oversaw the teachers coming into the country and had to register them. I told him that I'm the only teacher here and I was expecting a ride to my accommodation. I had no idea where I was staying. He told me to stay there and not to worry because someone was coming to pick me up. I hung up the phone and thanked the man. While I made the phone call, I was near the baggage claim. Everyone picked up their bags. I waited and waited and waited. I didn't see my bag. I went to the baggage claim office to ask where my luggage was, they told me it must've been stuck at the other location so they would have to get back to me when they get the chance to search in the computer to track it down. I had to wait for a long time at the airport until I can get an answer. I couldn't believe it! I had no bags, and my abaya was in my luggage. In the airport, I didn't see the women cover themselves that much, but I was worried about what would happen if I stepped out of the airport!

The man at the baggage claim office told me to come back the next day because my luggage was not there. They promised to track it down by the following day. This was a nightmare! I walked away and choose a spot at the airport to stand alone. I started to pray and said, "God, are you kidding me?" "Are you sure I'm supposed to be here?" If I was in South Korea, I think things would've run smoothly. I asked the Lord to please protect me and guide me through all this. In a few minutes, I saw a guy come in an EdEx uniform and I ran towards him and asked if he was here looking to pick up a teacher. He said, yes! I said, "Hallelujah! Praise God!" He didn't speak English that well, but he understood. I walked out with him, and a few people were staring because they noticed that I didn't have an abaya on, and I hopped in the van and sat next to the driver. Geez! The rules in this country! Interestingly, the driver was a good-looking guy. He was from Yemen. I had to learn that the women wearing a black abaya were important because they had to cover themselves so the men wouldn't be able to see their bodies. Men are known to be attracted to women's bodies. In Saudi Arabia, the color of the women's abaya must be black since it's a dark color and it's not easy for the man to see through. It makes sense why they chose black but took time for me to adjust because the sun during the day is scorching hot!

I finally made it to my destination without my luggage but at least I had my computer and my bag. I told the driver the situation with my luggage, but I don't think he understood. I went into the accommodation, and I was amazed. The lobby looked beautiful. The area didn't look fancy, but the accommodation looked pleasant. An American woman came down to greet me. I told her about my issue with the luggage and she was nice enough to let me use her abaya. I went to my room and was excited to see how beautiful it looked. I was also happy because I didn't have to room with anyone, and I wanted to experience what it would be like to have a room to myself for once. I felt so relieved! I started looking for plugs so I could connect my computer to e-mail people to let them know that I arrived safely in the Middle East. Ahhhhhh! It felt good!

I met some other teachers there and they were nice. I met one from South Africa, one from Somalia, and one later from Egypt. They were Muslim and were very nice and they made me feel comfortable because this was my first time in the Middle East teaching. They recommend that I go shopping for food. I was told to come with at least enough money to convert to 500 SAR which was 133 dollars in U.S. money. The other teachers thought that the amount was not going to be enough for me to survive until my first paycheck. One of the teachers offered to lend it to me and I could pay her back when we get paid. She was Somali. These teachers were nice.

There was a shopping bus that would come on certain days. There was a schedule in the lobby. The teacher asked if I wanted to go with them to go food shopping and I told them OK. I was lucky that one of the teachers gave me an abaya but there was one little problem. I didn't have a headscarf. One of the teachers asked if I had one but I told them I had to wait until the next day to pick up my luggage at the airport. We got on the shopping bus which was the EdEx bus, and we went to a shopping mall. I got out of the van and had an experience that made me so scared that I was ready to run back to the airport to go back home.

We went to the mall and bought food and other things since there were other stores in the mall. I'm so glad that I went. We all finished and went outside the mall to wait for the van to pick us up. As I was waiting, there were two men acting as if they were the police. They oversee making sure women and men have dressed appropriately. One of the men yelled at me and said, "You, Woman!" "Cover your head!" I was so scared because I had my abaya on, and I didn't have my scarf and hijab to cover my head. The other two teachers looked at me and said, "Ingrid!" "You can go to jail for that if you don't cover yourself." I was so scared and that's when I knew I wanted to go home. I was pacing back and forth waiting for the bus to come and get us. I was hoping for the bus to come quickly but the two men were coming back in our direction again. I was thinking what do I say?

One of the teachers said, "Ingrid, quickly!" "Hide behind one of the cars in the parking lot so they won't see you." "You'll get into trouble, and you can't just say you don't have a headscarf!"

The other teacher said, "You won't get in trouble because you're a foreigner. They wouldn't do that!"

The other teacher was arguing back stating, "Yes, she can get into trouble."

While these two teachers were arguing if I should hide or not, the men were coming closer. I figured since I'm in another country I better not take the risk, so I hurried to hide behind one of the cars in the parking lot. My heart was pounding so fast! I was thinking to myself, "God, you sent me here and I have to go to jail because I didn't cover my head?" "This doesn't make any sense." I waited quietly behind the car and one of the teachers started laughing and came to tell me that the coast is clear. Would you believe within minutes the bus finally came? I looked up in the air and said to God, "Whew!" That was a close call!" We got on the bus with our shopping bags and headed to our accommodation. I couldn't believe it and I had just come into the country. I went into my accommodation and was mesmerized by the setting. It was beautifully furnished and well decorated. It was a huge room. I was thinking to myself...wow! I finally have no roommate. I had the room all to myself.

I had the chance to meet other teachers and they were nice. Most of them were Muslims who were nice people. Most of the teachers were very smart. I had the experience to teach abroad in South Korea through the church, but I never had the experience to teach outside of the church. I knew this was going to be an interesting challenge. Within the week, school started, and the bus came and picked up all the teachers that needed to be at work. We had it arranged from the company we worked for which was EdEx and was sent to a Women's University. We had an orientation, and it also gave us an idea of what to do during the first week with the students since all of them hadn't registered yet. They gave us ideas about what to do since we didn't have books yet, so we had the chance to play games with the students. It was a pretty good idea to come up with some games for an English class because it was a chance for the students to open up and introduce themselves to each other.

Within two weeks, we were able to take attendance since there were deadlines for registration. I had the chance to introduce myself and I had the students each talk a little about themselves just to get an idea of how much English they knew. I liked my class because I was able to run it the way I wanted to. We later received the books and our schedules which enabled us to see when the exams, holidays, and study periods were. I was nervous because I was thinking about the teachers who have been teaching for years, while I just came off the Mission field. I had to really do it professionally. I had the chance to meet with other teachers to ask about their experience as a teacher in other schools. It was interesting to meet with other teachers from different cultures. I had some challenges but with some help from the other teachers, things ran smoothly. I began to observe that things would be a bit better if the teachers worked together a little more. It wasn't easy working with teachers who had different levels of experience, some that taught for years or who had higher credentials and wanted to be in charge and run things. I learned in Saudi Arabia that most women don't have much of a say. There were certain rules I had to learn while being here. Some of the rules I found to be extreme. I had to look up some of the rules online to make sure and to ask some of my Muslim friends to make sure I would survive safely.

What I learned is the following:

Don't leave home without your I.D. They issue a residency card which is called an iquama.

Muslims have their daily prayer five times a day. In Saudi Arabia, everything stops and shuts down for prayer which lasts 20-30 minutes each time.

Women must be dressed in abayas. When working in Saudi Arabia you must dress respectfully. Women must wear an abaya (long black dress/cloak covering the entire body) at all times outside, and they must cover their hair. It is good practice to always carry a headscarf.

It is illegal to have pornography.

All pork is banned. All pork products are illegal.

Unless you are married or a direct blood relative, you are not allowed to mix in private with someone of the opposite sex. If you're caught you might be jailed or deported.

If you have an affair, the penalty for adultery is death. I never saw a married couple kiss each other in public. Affection between men and women is not tolerated in public.

Do not swear or make obscene gestures. People are easily offended (or choose to be offended just to give you trouble) and things can escalate out of control.   If someone takes a dislike to you, remove yourself from the situation as quickly as possible. The general rule here is that a Saudi is always right. Even if you are in the "right" in a dispute, if the dispute is with a Saudi, you (as a foreigner) are wrong.

Women are not allowed to drive in Saudi Arabia; therefore, they must have a driver.

Alcohol is illegal. It's not allowed in the country not even in mouthwash and perfumes.

Drugs are illegal and the penalty is death.

Working in Saudi Arabia may seem very restrictive, but at the end of the day, we are here for the money and the lack of taxes. The punishment in Saudi is severe.

After looking this up on the internet I thought to myself, "Oh Lord, am I going to survive?" Strangely enough, I did make it through the year, and with some help from the other teachers, it wasn't so bad. I've realized what made it easy was that I was so busy working that I did not have too much time to think about the rules. It gave me an opportunity to learn about their culture. Their religion is interesting, but I knew that God didn't send me there to become a Muslim. We were not allowed to speak about religion, politics, birthdays, opposite sex, drugs, or sex in the classroom. When we had our breaks, a few students would ask if I was Muslim, and they would give me a pamphlet and talk to me about it outside of class. I would tell the students that if I was going to learn about their religion then they should learn about mine since I'm a Christian because God wants us to respect each other.

I came to learn that Muslims all over the world come to do their holy pilgrimage to Mecca, which is one of their pillars of the Islamic faith. They worship at the Kaaba. I didn't even know that the Kaaba was in Saudi Arabia! I was thinking, "God, you got to be kidding me. " I asked GOD what is my purpose since you told me not to marry a Muslim. God said to me, "Just tell them about who Jesus is." I was thinking to myself that I'm going to get killed since I found out all these rules. God would want us to respect one another so why should the Muslims feel like they would have to punish me? I found out later we're not allowed to protest or even spread information about Jesus in the open.

I figured, let me get to know a little about their religion and then they can learn about mine but discreetly. I was not allowed to have long conversations with the students, but I had the chance to speak with the teachers because some of them wanted me to be converted. I learned about the Kaaba in Mecca which made me wonder why the Muslims kept walking around it in prayer. I found out that non-Muslims are not allowed to worship there. I told the Muslims that's extreme because in Israel we're allowed to have all religions visit Gethsemane. I asked questions about their Qur'an, and they asked me questions about the Bible. I found out why the Kaaba was important to them, and it was interesting to know because Abraham and Ishmael were also in our Bible. Muslims believe that the Kaaba was built by Adam when Allah sent him to earth with his wife Eve/ Hawa. The house was then rebuilt by Abraham and his elder son Ishmael to worship Allah, the only God but over time it became the most important and most sacred religious site of Arab Pagans who worshipped 360 idols of Gods and Goddesses inside the house. It became an annual pilgrimage site of all Arab Mushrik pagans and a business hub for them. Kaaba became the biggest trade hub of the Arab peninsula. Prophet Mohammad got the revelation from the Abrahamic God, called Allah. This God is also worshipped by Christians and Jews call him Yahweh. He was also the main God of Arab Mushriks along with several other gods then Muhammad and his followers entered inside the Kaaba and demolished all pagan idols and dedicated the house solely to worship Allah. It then became an important ritual for Muslims to perform tawaf(circulation) seven times around the black house (Kaaba) and sacrifice a domestic animal in the name of Allah. Every year, millions of Muslims travel to Mecca for the hajj, umrah, one of the five pillars of the Islamic faith. Muslims travel to Islam's most sacred mosque, al-Masjid al-Haram, during the six-day pilgrimage. Mecca is thought to be the place where Ishmael and his mother Hagar were provided with a spring of water in the desert.

I started to tell the teachers about my beliefs as a Christian. I told the Muslim teachers that we are called Christians because we are followers of Christ. Jesus to us is the son of God. We believe that

Jesus is the son of God since God is spirit. I found out the Muslims heard who Jesus is but does everyone around the world know who the prophet Muhammad is? Islam seemed to be the largest growing religion at this present time as I noticed watching it on the news. It was nice to sit down with the teachers and exchange our beliefs but there were a few of them that were a bit annoyed because they wanted me to convert right away. I was a bit intimidated and a bit scared because I was afraid that the Muslim teachers would report me. Strangely enough, most of the teachers were still willing to guide me and show me around the school. I kept on remembering how you're not allowed to have Bibles or try to convert others into Christianity, but they were nice to hear about our beliefs as Christians. I'm glad I had the chance to explain as Christians we respect other religions, and we give out pamphlets to let readers learn about the way of Christ. In the long run, I had told them that Jesus showed us how to act among other people so we would demonstrate it. I told them why don't you show me an example of how the prophet Muhammad showed the Muslims how they treat one another? I noticed that they got quiet and then one teacher said, "Ok, we'll show you."

I mentioned also that wouldn't God want us to respect each other since God is love?

One of the teachers said, "Yes."

I said, "Well then, let's represent God." They all smiled and said, "Ok."

Later we continued to go to our offices and start our paperwork. I started meeting some more teachers and made some more friends later. We as God's people started to respect each other even more. Our interactions led to more and more teachers listening to sermons on TV and coming to me to learn about God from a Christian perspective. It worked! I had the chance to even show a program with Oprah interviewing DeVon Franklin as he was explaining about the Sabbath. He saved my life because I was worried if I was going to get into trouble if I mentioned the word Jesus but miraculously the teachers became more interested! Thank you, Jesus! More teachers started to come to my office and were curious about my beliefs. We exchanged our beliefs and we respected each other because we realized that's what God would want us to do. I don't think God would approve of us fighting! We wouldn't represent God if we did that!

Teaching at a university was interesting but it took a lot of adjusting for me. I was afraid at first because I met teachers who were very experienced. Some taught for many years, and some had PhDs and Master's Degrees. I like the fact that it was always a learning experience and there were teachers that helped each other. We even had sessions to help enhance our teaching abilities. It was fun learning different ideas from other teachers. Some teachers are better than others and some were in the process of learning. I liked the environment in that aspect, but I didn't like the environment when you're being micro-managed or bullied.

There were other odd things I experienced but I just kept it to myself. As I walked around the campus, I noticed that there were a few dead birds. I wondered if it was normal or if there was something in the air. I just kept quiet and then I realized a teacher brought up the same scenario to me. I realized I wasn't the only one who noticed it. I was trying to wonder why every time I walked outside the campus, I've noticed there were a few dead birds on the ground. I was wondering is this normal to see this on a regular. Teachers who had PhDs and Master's Degrees.

The students at the university in Saudi Arabia were not too bad. The students in Saudi Arabia are a bit laid back compared to the students from South Korea. The students were friendly. The students from South Korea had more freedom to show the teachers around. The Saudi students surprised me with a cake of appreciation as a teacher at the University. I was a little shocked considering that we were not allowed to have parties. It gave me a chance to see how the Arab students are. There were prayer times that were scheduled so I would respect the students for them to go for prayer. I respect Muslims for their prayer times because at least they make the time for God. There was one student I remembered who gave me a Qur'an as a gift and it can be translated as I listened to it. It was neat. She always wanted me to become a Muslim and I would always say to her I will read your Qur'an if you read my Bible. I didn't have the Bible of course but I would tell her she could look online, and I would tell her to look at the story about Jesus of Nazareth on YouTube. I would tell her that God wants us to get along with each other and not fight. God is going to judge everyone regardless of our religion. It's important to understand each other, learn from one another, respect each other, and pray for one another. God is love so you should represent God. I told her as Christians that what was taught to us. The prophet Mohammad also taught her that one shouldn't kill or force people to join a religion. It's not of God.

The students needed to adjust to being in school the entire day because of how the system was set up. Many of the students had dreams and goals. Some wanted to go into social work, become a nurse, a doctor, a teacher and some even wanted to go into computers. I met some nice students and some not-so-nice ones, but it taught me to realize that not everyone is perfect. In South Korea, the students respect their teachers and are more determined. I still had fun with some of the students in Saudi because some of them loved to learn about different cultures and they loved to meet people. It's beautiful to see that in their culture.

I also witnessed another strange incident at this university. All the teachers were set in a group. I had about four teachers in a group and each of us had to give a presentation. I remembered when it was my turn, I couldn't move my slides. I hit the enter button and it wouldn't go to the next slide. I was pressing hard on the button, and it wouldn't go to the next slide. I was pressing hard on the button, and it still didn't move. It was really strange and then my friend who went before me came and said, "Bismila" which means in the name of God and then it went to the next slide. I thought to myself I should have said, "In the name of Jesus" and it would have moved to the next slide. When it happened, I noticed everyone was staring at me like they were perplexed or intimidated. They were trying to figure out how or why did that happen. My friend decided to handle the slides and I just delivered my presentation. When our group finished everyone clapped. We clapped for all the groups because all the teachers did a wonderful job. When that little incident took place with the slides, I later looked for a classroom and sat by myself.

I started to think about how every time I wanted to get things done when the manager asked me to hand in my work at a certain time things would go wrong. There wasn't a problem with the manager, but it must have been a technical problem with the computer. It's not like I did things on purpose, but it just wouldn't go smoothly sometimes. I remember I had to get some documents in at a certain time and I got it in early. The manager would contact me and say, "Ingrid, I haven't received your paperwork." It was weird because I would look at my sent log on my computer and notice it did go through. I would bring my computer to the office and show proof that I sent in the documents. She would show it to me on her end that she didn't receive it. I would resend it again in front of her and sometimes she got it and sometimes she did not. I sometimes wondered if God wanted to remind me that I needed to remember my mission; to show an example of how Christians should behave and remember to remind them who Jesus was. I had some weird experiences working at the university but at least I was able to meet some wonderful people. It was not easy to decipher who were your real friends. I started to learn the fewer friends the better.

I started to e-mail a few friends back home with some of my experiences, but I couldn't get into detail because I realized maybe someone is checking into my emails. I realized it's been three years since I've been in Saudi Arabia and things started to change.

In Saudi Arabia they started to incorporate taxes, they cut the salaries from a lot of employees, and little by little they are going to let foreigners leave the country. The good news is that they are now allowing women to drive. This happened as soon as I left the country in September of 2017. I'm not sure but it seems like they're trying to generate money for their country. I'm a little confused as to why since the country has a lot of oil. I sometimes wondered what would happen if their oil ran out. It was already tough when there was a war with Yemen they had to come up with the costs for a war. I also heard that it was estimated that 50,000 Sudanese left Saudi Arabia. It seemed like something was about to take place that not too many people were happy about. I'm not sure in detail but it seems like Saudi Arabia is trying to build up their economy. It was fun to experience a different country and a different culture. It's still peaceful there because it's considered a religious country. The rules are a bit strict, but it works for what that country represents. It was easy for me to adjust because I was occupied in my job. If I hadn't worked there, it would have been difficult for me to adjust because I'm used to the freedom in my country.

I would tell people if they want to come to Saudi make sure they learn the rules before they decide to visit the country or else you will be in for a surprise. I later realized many teachers were leaving my accommodation and going home. I started to get nervous because I wanted to know why so many teachers are leaving. I started to pray, and God told me that it was time to leave. I wondered how I was going to leave when I needed an exit visa. You needed permission from the country to leave. I signed the contract to end the job, but I felt perplexed because I needed to see if I was going to get my bonus pay and resettlement money before I left the country. I waited and waited but no bonus pays and resettlement. One of my friends from Egypt decided to go to Mecca. She came back and received bad news. She had to leave due to a family emergency. She contacted me quickly and told me to come with her to do the paperwork. She advised me to leave the country also. We went to the office and did our paperwork and booked our flights. I didn't know why the company we worked for too long gave us our bonus and resettlements, but it made me realize it was probably due to the changes that were taking place in Saudi. It was time for me to head home. I also wanted to obey God since He said it's time to go back to the U.S. God's timing is always perfect. When you put God first everything falls into place.

CHAPTER 9

I'M COMING HOME!

While I was in Saudi Arabia, I booked my ticket and then waited until it was time to leave the country. I was thinking to myself which place I should visit first since I have family members in different places. My ticket was set for me to leave the country in September. It was already the end of July going into August and I realized it was time to start boxing everything since I decided to leave permanently. In the meantime, in Saudi, I did a lot of prayer and reflection on what I've been through. When I connected with the Saudi students, I've had the chance to see how they interact with each other and how God is very important in their life. I respected that highly. I admired the fact that they take the time to pray to God five times a day which in Arabic is called Salah. They shut down every store for Salah. It's amazing! I also believe you can pray to God anytime but at least when two or three are gathered to pray there is power in prayer. I'm glad I had the chance to exchange my beliefs with a few of the Muslim teachers because it gave me a chance to learn about their religion and their culture. I was happy to find that there are some beautiful Muslims in this world. I've learned that they know who Jesus is and they know that Jesus is a good person. I prayed and I remembered God told me to just tell them about Jesus. In the process, I figured out that I had to show them what Jesus would do in certain situations. Jesus taught us to love and respect each other. I even showed them a few videos of Jesus's interaction with the sinners and how he treated them. I've learned that we may look different, we may speak a different language, our religions are different, but God would want us to love each other despite our differences. They showed me about their Prophet Muhammad, and I realized his teachings are not bad. According to Islamic doctrine, he was a Prophet. I've met some wonderful teachers and they gave me a chance to experience their culture. What we all learned is that no matter what we are all God's creation and God would want us to love each other because God is love. Being in Saudi gave me a chance to get closer to God and to pray more. I had the chance to see the Muslims celebrate their holidays. It was beautiful. I had the chance to explain about the Sabbath and what we do in church and how we fellowship as Christians. It was beautiful for us to exchange our beliefs and to respect each other. I had the chance to pray every day and I had asked God,

"Ok, where should I go next?" I was excited to find out because I wanted to see what my next mission was. God said, "Go home and meet with your family and friends." "Do something else, write a book about your journey with me."

I said, "What?" "God, I don't know how to write a book."

God said, "Go home and write then I will tell you what to do next."

It felt as if I just go where the wind blows. My life belongs to God. Well, at least I will know what to do but I won't know where to go. Not yet! Each day passed and I stayed most of the time in my apartment praying and started writing. It was getting closer to the time of departure. I had so many people to visit that I had no idea as to where I should visit first since I couldn't make it for the summer in July. I had plans to visit my family from the Northwest in the summer but because I had to wait to see if I was going to receive resettlement it messed up my program. I decided to visit my family from the

North then visit my other family relatives later. I contacted one of my relatives from the North who happens to have some connections with some important people, and I told one of them that I'm going to stop by and visit you all first. He wanted to know if I was hired by a Saudi company or an American company. I told him I was hired by a Saudi Company. I told him I still didn't receive my resettlement or my vacation pay. He was wondering what was happening and then he said OK just come and I'll meet you at the airport.

The day finally arrived so I just finished packing my things and it was time to go to the airport. I was still checking my e-mail to see if they mentioned anything about my vacation pay and resettlement. Nada! Well, I received a call at my apartment from downstairs in the lobby and they mentioned the cab is here. I hurried and grabbed all my belongings and rushed to the lobby. I gave a tip to the helpers who helped with my luggage, and I just jumped right into the cab. I made it to the airport and realized I have a layover in Italy. When I got to the airport I went through the procedures, and I made it to the airline's check-in desk. They told me at the check-in desk that you must pick up your luggage claim area at my layover if it's not my destination. They just told me it's airline procedures. I didn't argue so I checked in my luggage then went to the gate. I sat for about an hour then it was time to board. Bon Voyage Saudi! I got on the plane, sat at my seat, prayed, and then relaxed. It was soon time for take-off and realized it was the end of Saudi for now. I relaxed on the plane and watched a film called "The Kingsman 2 Golden Circle." After the movie, I relaxed and went to sleep. Hours went to the baggage claim check area and waited for about 20 minutes and realized my luggage wasn't there. I quickly ran to the gate where I was supposed to check in then looked for the gate to board. The ladies at the boarding check-in said, "Ingrid Apollon?"

I said, "Yes, that's me!"

The desk clerk said, "Ma'am, we paged you to board the plane!"

"Now the plane has taken off!"

I said, "I was told that my luggage was going to be at the baggage claim!"

They looked it up and said, "Ingrid, your luggage is here!" I said, "They told me to go to a particular office to pick up the luggage." I ran to the office and saw my suitcases. I was so upset. I went to the information desk and asked when the next flight to the USA. They said, there is only one flight today so the next one is tomorrow." "Great!" "Now, I'm stuck in Italy!" I had to look for a payphone so I can call my relatives to tell them I'm not going to come until tomorrow. I finally found a payphone but no response, so I left a message stating that my flight was tomorrow. I walked around the airport to look for an information booth and asked if there was a hotel. They told me the closest one is the Hilton Hotel across the street. I had a few suitcases that were heavy, so I had to haul them on the cart and push it all the way to the hotel. It was a long walk to the hotel. I've noticed the security guard in front of the hotel. He was nice enough to open the door for me I said, "Hello."

I noticed he has an accent, so it was not from the United States. It sounded like one of the countries from Africa. When I got to the hotel, I asked the woman behind the check-in desk if she accepts American dollars. She told me no. I asked if they knew a place where I can convert my money. She then told me that I would have to go to the airport. I've noticed behind their desk that there were some suitcases in a small room. I had asked if I can leave my cart of luggage so I can walk all the way back to the airport. One staff member had mentioned to me that we can't accept any suitcases.

I looked at him and said, "Why not?" "I see you have other suitcases in the room." "I just need a place to leave it temporarily because this is a lot of suitcases to push all the way back to the airport. It's too far of a walk."

He said, "I'm sorry Ma'am" "You will have to take the suitcases with you."

I was so upset but I decided not to argue and just go. While I was talking with one of the staff about the issue, I've noticed the African security guard glanced from a distance and witnessed the argument. He saw me push the cart and he ran ahead of me to open the door.

I said, "Thank you."

I walked all the way back to the airport with the cart of luggage to look for a place to exchange the American dollars for Euros. I walked all the way back to the hotel with the cart and realized the security guard was not in front of the hotel. I looked through the glass door and realized a tall black man was arguing with the staff member who told me that I couldn't leave my luggage in the room behind the front desk. I opened the door and suddenly there was silence. I pushed the cart towards the front desk and a few of the staff members came to help me unload the cart. The staff at the check-in all apologized to me and recommended that I stay in one of their large suites. I don't know what happened, but I realized all the staff members were extremely nice to me. The security guard smiled at me while all the other staff members were extremely nice to him. I wonder if he was getting promoted. I didn't even see the tall African American man. It's like he disappeared. I have no idea where he went. I finally checked into my room and made a phone call to connect with my family. One of my relatives answered the call so I was happy I didn't get the answering machine. I told him the whole story. He was shocked to hear I was stuck in Italy but at least I'm safe. I checked-in in the afternoon after all that fiasco and I just rested. I got up in the evening and went for a walk to look for a restaurant to eat at. I went all the way back to the airport and ordered a chicken Caesar salad then took it back to my hotel room. I ate and it was getting late, so I went to bed since my flight was in the morning. I just remembered my flight was before 12 p.m. I had called for a wake-up call down at the front desk.

It was the next day, and it was time to finish quickly packing and head to the airport. I was so happy that the hotel was near the airport. Surprisingly, one of the staff members came and asked if I needed help with the luggage. I told them sure I would really appreciate it. One of them asked would I like for them to assist with the cart of luggage to the airport. I told them it was ok. It's amazing how nice they are now suddenly. I have a feeling they felt guilty after the way they treated me. I had a feeling the tall African American man who spoke to the staff members must've been an important person. I've learned that you should always treat people nice in customer service because if you treat them badly now, you may regret it later in the future. One day, you'll look back and realize the same person you had treated badly may become a CEO later in the future. You just never know! It's important to treat people nicely. I had two bottles of water and offered one to the security guard.

He smiled and said, "No it's ok." "It was a pleasure to meet you and have a safe trip." I pushed my cart and made it to the airport and went to the check-in desk to check my luggage. It was smooth sailing from there. It was soon time to board the plane and I made it on time. It was time for the plane to take off and I was on my way to see my family. I rested most of the time on the plane. It was soon time to land, and I was on my way to baggage claim and spotted one of my relatives. He looked great and I told him I had a safe flight. He contacted the rest of the family members to let them know that I made it safely back to the USA.

He drove me to my aunt's house, and we parked the car and got out to ring the doorbell. She opened the door and she hugged me and my cousin. She was so happy to see us. We all sat down, and she offered dinner. We all caught up and talked. She was so excited to see me and was excited to also hear about my experience overseas in Saudi Arabia. After dinner, it was soon time for my cousin to leave since he had an appointment. My aunt and I hugged him and thanked him for picking me up from the airport. I later explained to her what happened in Italy with the layover. She had told me about her situation on how she can't walk much so she uses the cane a lot and she drives most of the time. I told her I know how to drive so I could take her places if she needed to. We talked about church and what there is to do out here in her area. There was a train close by but no stores close by. I would drive her to church every Sunday and take her shopping. I told her I had plans to stay for a month since I had to rearrange my plans. She told me it would be perfect because she had to go on vacation the following month. I stayed with her for the whole month of September. I contacted one of my relatives from the Northwest to let them know I will come to visit next month. We had a good time together catching up. It gave me a chance to discuss the family and my next plans. It was interesting to hear about the stories in the past with the family, but it gave me a chance to try to understand why some family members get along and why some don't. What family doesn't have conflicts? It wouldn't be normal if all the family members didn't get along, but we all love each other.

I just realized that we're all older and everyone is mostly busy doing their own thing. What hits me the most is that most of the family members have gotten married and have kids. I haven't even gotten married yet and I'm in my forties. It really hit me as I witnessed all of them are busy living their lives. As for me, my life belongs to God, and I just go where he takes me. I had the chance to meet some other relatives and had a chance to visit my other aunt. The two aunts didn't live too far from each other. I had a great time. I had the chance to visit some parks, malls, visit their seaport, visit her church, and eat at different restaurants. I even had the chance to celebrate one of my aunt's birthdays. I took a lot of photos, and I was so happy to see how beautiful it is. I had the chance to visit. I had such a great time that I realized time was flying and it was soon time for me to visit my family from the Northwest. At the end of the month came to visit my family from the Northwest. The end of the month came so fast. You know the saying "Time flies when you're having fun!" I already know if I don't make my way to visit the other family members, I won't hear the end of it. One group of the family will say, "How come she went to visit them and not us?" Another family group may say, "Well she didn't even tell us where she is." Etc…etc…etc… You know how family can be. It's normal. It was time to contact my family from the Northwest and the Northeast. I told them I'm coming to town in October, and they were pleased and excited. I packed my things and said my goodbyes to all my relatives from the North. They gave me the advice to see if I can stay in the U.S. to work but I told them I'm still praying and waiting to see where God wants me to go next. God comes first. The family from the North suggested seeing what I can do to help my brother also. I told them it was not going to be easy because I'm not in a predicament to help him now. I'm not married, I have no house, no car, and for now no job. I'm just following God's orders. It reminded me how God told me to do something else and work on my book. They told me to at least go and visit. I told them of course no problem. It was time to make my visits, so my flight was booked on my way to the airport. I went to the check-in desk and had no problem. It was smooth sailing. I made it to the gates, waited, and soon it was time for me to board the plane. I got on the plane, sat, and relaxed. It was soon time for take-off. As I waited for the take-off and felt good about my visit to the North, God told me it was not meant for me to stay there.

Northwest Here I come!

I rested most of the time on the plane and it was a shorter distance from Italy to the east. It was about seven hours, so I had the chance to rest again. It was soon time to land, and I got excited since this was home. I was thinking to myself that Northwest is where I'm living now. As far as Northeast, I no longer live there since God told me to leave but there's no going back. It's a place I will always have in my heart to visit but to go back and live it's over. I'm glad as a family we had the chance to resolve our issues. It does sound a bit weird to say but God told me to run away from home, which was in the Northeast at that time, but I had no choice. My life belongs to the Lord now and it was time to move forward and receive the blessings God has in store for me. While my mind was racing with excitement thinking about my destinations, the plane was soon preparing for landing. I got off the plane and went to baggage claim and got my luggage then looked for a phone to call one of my cousins. He told me to wait at the baggage claim and he will come to the airport to get me. I waited for about 15 minutes, and he came in. He came in with his wife and his brother. We all hugged each other. We got to our destination, and we all got out of the car in peace. I walked in saying, "I'm home!" My little niece came to the door and smiled. I hugged her realizing how big she had gotten. The family met me at the door, and we all hugged each other. We had the chance to connect and talk about our updates and what everyone has been up to. Everyone was busy and doing what they had to do. It's October so I had to think about how to schedule in to visit my family from the Northeast. I decided to take a trip on Thanksgiving and that will give me a chance to see everyone. The beauty of this trip is that it's only four hours away so I can just hop on the bus. I had the chance to see some people around the neighborhood and get to do some things.

There is a church I attend all the time there which is a Seventh Day Adventist church. I was able to get back in time to visit and see the pastor. My favorite part of the church is attending Wednesday night prayer meetings. I'm glad I had the chance to catch up with the church family. During my stay at Northwest, I started to do some writing to focus on the book. It wasn't easy because there were a lot of distractions with pets, my niece, and my relatives walking in and out, so I had to figure out a schedule. I had the chance to speak to them about Saudi. They looked at the news and realized it's best to stay put in the U.S. for a while with all the changes taking place in Saudi. I had time to attend restaurants, go to the movies, the malls, parties and etc.... with the family. I had the chance to contact my brother who's in the Northeast and contact the family there also. I even called a couple of close friends to let them know I'm in the U.S. and I will be visiting them soon. Time was flying again when you were having fun and it was soon time to go to the family from the Northeast. I booked my bus trip online and contacted my cousin who lived in the upper region from the Northeast. He worked in the city, so it was easy for me to book a bus ride since the bus station was located there. I decided to book it near November since Thanksgiving was approaching so I can spend time with them for the holidays. It was time to go so I finished asking and gave big hugs to the family from the Northwest. I told them that I will be back soon. I hopped on the bus and made it smoothly to the city. I called one of my relatives and told him I made it and I'm here. Surprisingly, his car was right across the street. He waved and gave me a hug then came to help me with my luggage to put them in his car. I called my family from the Northwest to let them know I made it safely.

We made it safely and I greeted everyone. I had a great time with the family. We went to the movies, went to visit the mall, went to the motorcycle show, and even had a chance to see the kids go trick-or-treating. During my stay, I had some quiet time while the kids were in school, and I went full speed ahead to continue writing my book. Time flew by again and it was time to visit some friends, so I hopped on the train and made my visits. What was so cool was that I had the chance to travel back and forth from the upper North Region to the Northeast anytime. Thanksgiving was approaching so I had contacted the family from the Northeast to see if they wanted me to make anything I didn't make anything, but I decided to buy sodas. Thanksgiving Day came and it was time for us to drive to the Northeast. There were other family members in town that came and brought some dishes too. We made it safely to the Northeast and had the chance to hug each other and catch up on old times. I had the chance to tell them the story about my experience overseas but as far as my next move I had to wait on God. We all had fun at the dinner table and had a great time telling funny stories. I had the chance to catch up with my brother and my aunt. We're cool but it's now time for all of us to get ourselves together and grow. It's cool that we resolve our issues but what came to mind was when Ms. Queen told me about how God told me to leave the Northeast and my life belongs to God now. There's no going back to live there. I love to travel and meet people, but God knows he always uses me in his plans. I love that. I know that He will protect me, provide for me and profess for me. I may not be rich materialistically to what God told me to do first which was to work on my project. Thanksgiving was fun and it gave all of us a chance to get together. I still had the chance to still contact my family from the North by phone, so everyone is ok. It was time for me to head back to the upper North region with my family. We all hugged each other, and we all went our separate ways.

Each family member is doing their best to work hard. As for me, it's time to continue God's path and do for myself. Someone once told me how you can take care of anyone if you can't even take care of yourself. I thought about it and that person brought up a good point! I can't take care of myself. My aunt from up North suggested you should think about getting married. One day I will but in God's time. One of my other cousins suggested not to look for a man. I wasn't even looking! I was too busy focusing on my job overseas. As for now, God wants me to work on writing the book. Well, we made it back safely to the upper region and I continued writing. The holidays were coming up, so I needed to soon head back to Northwest where I lived. I realized I had another friend I had to visit down South. I booked my flight before Christmas, so I had plans to stay for a week. I contacted my family from Northwest and told them I will be flying south to make sure my friend is ok. They understood because they remembered I usually make my rounds to visit people. I started packing and it was time to get to the airport. I gave my hugs goodbye. It's December and I realized it's cold and snowy. I called for a cab and made it to the airport smooth sailing. I checked in my bags and made it to the gate on time. It was soon time to board the plane and so far, everything is great! It was only a three-hour ride to the South. The plane took off and I rested. We just had snacks on the plane since it was a short ride. It was about close to three hours. It was fast. It was soon time to land. We landed and I contacted my friend to let her know that I arrived. She told me it's ok the driver will meet you. I got off the plane and made it through towards baggage claim. I see a tall dark-skinned man with glasses wearing a black trench coat waving at me. He came up to me with his Caribbean accent.

Are you Ingrid?

I said, "Yes, how did you know?"

He said, "Your friend told me what you were wearing." "Here let me help you with your luggage." I got in the car, and we made it safely to her house. I thanked the driver for picking me up from the airport. I saw her in front of the house, and we hugged each other hello. She looked great! I had the chance to see her son and he looked great! I walked into her house, and we caught up on good times. It was nice down South considering that the weather was warm compared to the upper North Region. It was evening time, so I was getting tired and wanted to catch up on some shuteye. I thank God for good friends. I went to the room where she wanted me to stay which was nice. I told her to thank you for sending me the driver. We said our goodnights and went to our rooms. I prayed and I heard God's voice. "Ingrid, finish your book."

I said, "Yes, Lord I will.

It was the next day and we had breakfast then went for a ride. She started to show me parts of down South. I had a chance to visit the malls, go to the restaurants, go to the movies and go indoor skydiving. It was soon time to head home since the time went so fast. I booked my flight so I can head back to Northwest. I called my family to let them know I was coming to make it for Christmas. I watched the news and saw there was a snowstorm coming. Most of the flights got canceled. I couldn't believe it! I had to call and change my booking. I pushed it for another week. My friend told me it's ok Ingrid you can stay here if you like. Thank God for good friends. I called my family from Northwest and told them I can't come. I'll come next week. Well, at least I had the chance to stay longer and meet some of her friends. I had a chance to even attend some house parties. I had the chance to go to concerts too. The week went by, and God reminded me to do the book. I was trying to finish it up then suddenly it was time to leave. Time flies when you're having fun. I looked at the news just to check and noticed there was a power outage at the airport! Most of the flights got canceled. I couldn't believe it! I contacted my family and realized I'm not coming. I called the flight and realized I might as well cancel. I didn't understand what was going on. Every time I wanted to head back; my flight got canceled. I started to think about how God wanted me to write a book. It looks like I won't make it back in time for Christmas.

It was time to pray but the beauty about all of this was that I had peace and quiet. If I went back to Northwest I probably would've been distracted because of my niece, the dogs, the people coming in and out, etc... It was close to Christmas, and I realized it was time for me to just accept I won't be spending Christmas with the family. It was ok so I just decided to stay and get gifts and celebrated the holiday with my friend from down South. Christmas came and we had a chance to spend time together. I had the chance to call all the family members for Christmas. I told them the situation and they understood but they were happy that at least I had the chance to visit. It was soon time for New Year's, and it was approaching. I looked at the weather channel and was told a winter storm was approaching. One of my nephews connected with me and asked, "Auntie, when are you coming back?"

I just got quiet and said, "I don't know, and I don't want to say anything anymore." "I'll just wait until the weather gets better. Love you." I hung up the phone and started to think about how God wanted me to write the book. Could it be that God is pulling me away from everyone so I wouldn't get any distractions? Interestingly, down South is peaceful and quiet. My friend contacted one of my other friends from high school and told me that she was getting married, but we had to keep it quiet. The wedding will take place in Jamaica. I guess I'm going to a wedding in Jamaica! I've always dreamed about white sands and blue waters. It's amazing! I'm living my dreams. I guess I'll stay down South for New Year's and will stay down South until it's time to go to Jamaica for our friend's wedding. It was New Year's and I called everyone for the holiday. I connected with one of my friends from High School who was getting married, and she insisted on me coming to her wedding. I was contemplating if I should go or not because I had to budget. My friend who I was visiting down South insisted that I should go. I prayed and God told me to go but remember do your book. It was near the time of the wedding, and we were all getting ready to pack. I had to remember that we had to keep this a secret so we couldn't tell anyone. I was so excited because I'd dreamed of vacationing on an island. It was time to hop on the plane and go. The flight from down South to Jamaica was smooth and relaxing. We landed with no problems. The staff who oversaw the wedding met up with us at the airport and welcomed us to Jamaica. We made it to the Resort, and it was called RIU Montego Bay Resort. The staff was very welcoming. We decided to check-in at the hotel, and everything was included. It was sweet! The only issue was that it didn't have any wi-fi in our rooms. You had to go to the lobby or go outside to get free Wi-Fi. We stayed for about a week. It was well coordinated. Everyday there was some activity and there wasn't a dull moment. They had Reggae Night, different restaurants, a tour of the town, swimming with the dolphins, a pool, and even the beautiful ocean. We even went on the paddle boats. Jamaica was beautiful. I even had the chance to walk alone on the beach. I met a few nice men but for some reason, God shut the door. I would always bump into them when they were connected with the women. Every night I would pray and thank the Lord for the opportunity to take a vacation. It just stopped.

The Lord was reminding me to do my book. It started to get a little weird. I remembered my friends and I went to Reggae Night to watch a concert. I had a virgin Pina Colada in my hand and was on my way to my seat then there were two guys from our wedding party was coming towards me so they can sit next to me. I accidentally spilled the drink on the chairs next to me and they couldn't sit there. They had to sit further away from me. I looked in the sky to God and said, "Are you kidding me?" God said, "Remember to do your book."

After the concert, I told the group that I'm going to go to my room and rest. I had my cell phone, and I was listening to some music. As I got to my room the Wi-Fi stopped so I just restarted my phone. I remembered once you get to the room there is no Wi-Fi. I turned on my phone and something strange happened. A video popped up about book publishing. It was about 1 minute and 26 seconds long. I hit play and was able to see the whole video. I was thinking to myself how did that happen if there was no Wi-Fi in the room? I was thinking to myself, "God you got to be kidding!" I went to open the door to check outside to see if there was a switch or something and there was nothing and no one was there. I closed my door and started to play another video and there was nothing. I just stopped. I couldn't believe it! It was strange. I went out to the balcony and started to pray because that freaked me out and I heard God's voice say, "Remember to write your book."

My mouth dropped. It was getting late so one of my friends made it back and I told her the story of what happened with my cell phone. She was amazed and was in shock. She was thinking how was that possible? I told her I don't know. She checked her cell phone and there was no Wi-Fi. We both looked at each other with astonishment. She looked at me and said, "You better start your book." "If God told you to do something you better do it."

It was late so it was time to get some shut eye because the next day was the rehearsal for the wedding. It was morning and we all met together and had breakfast then we had the rehearsal I even remembered bumping into a pastor who was from an Adventist church. I was thinking to myself no matter where I go across the world I will always bump into an Adventist. An Adventist is another Christian denomination. We are Christians who follow the Sabbath. It was soon time for the wedding. We all got dressed and my friend's son became the ring bearer, the flower girls were adorable! Everyone at the wedding looked marvelous! The bride and the groom looked amazing! The wedding was beautiful then after we had a day or two to enjoy the resort so the rest of our stay, we went to the pool and enjoyed relaxing by the ocean. It was time to soon head back to the South. The whole wedding party hugged each other goodbye and went their separate ways. As for me, God had bigger plans! It was time for me to head back and write my book.

My friend looked at me and said, "Ingrid, it's ok you can stay as long as you like." I thanked her because I knew God was pushing me to a place with no distractions and I needed to start writing about my journey with him. We got to the airport safely. We boarded the plane safely but sat separately. It was a smooth ride and we landed safely from Jamaica to the South. We felt like we were on a high from Jamaica because it was beautiful. We had a blast! Our driver came to pick us up from the airport and he noticed we looked stress-free. We made it safely to the house and it was time for all of us to get some shut-eye since it was nighttime. I got up the next morning and prayed then God reminded me to write the book. There are times that I realize I don't have a choice. My life belongs to God right now. He loves me and he knows what's best for me. He's my provider and my way maker. It felt as if God was nudging me to get it done. When God tells you to do something you have to do it. You must trust him and act. Sometimes he may ask you to do something, and it doesn't make sense, but my life belongs to God now. Yup! Sometimes I feel like living like a gypsy because I'm traveling all over the place but at least I have God as my compass. You must trust and obey. You must be still and listen to that quiet voice so you can hear him. How do I hear him and how do I know it's him? Once you read the bible and get to know his character you will know. For my next journey, I would have to just continue to listen to God and he will lead the way. I will later explain how I was able to discern his voice.

CHAPTER 10

GOD IS THAT YOU?

How did I discern God's voice? How did I know if it was really him? I don't know because I'm still going through the process. I'm not perfect at it but one thing I know is you will hear it clearly. How do I know? Well, for starters I usually read the Scripture for the day. I pray every day and have conversations with God. I usually read and get to know God. I start wondering how we started as human beings. How did God communicate with people in the past? Does God still do the same things as He did long ago? Does, he gets happy? Does he get angry? Does he love us? Does he give us free will? How will I know the answers to all these questions? Easy! Get to know him! It's like a relationship. How will you know about anyone if you don't get to know them? How can you say anything about a person if you don't get to know anyone yourself? Sometimes, there are people who want to know about celebrities for example, so they usually read magazines. If you want to know what's happening in the news, then you must read about it and watch it right? It's the same as you getting to know God. You must read about the people in the past who lived during the time when God was setting things up. You must make time for each other like a relationship. As I said, I'm not a pro and I still have a lot to learn! When you are part of God's plan, you are going to hear the voice of God.

I remember watching the movie, The Ten Commandments and I was so fascinated by God's power. I was amazed at how he made the sea turn red and how Moses' rod turned into a cobra and how the cobra ate the Pharaoh's other cobras. I was amazed because God was demonstrating how powerful He can be. He proved that no one can be above him because He is God. He was demonstrating His power as God. I loved how He split the Red Sea. I was in awe of His power. If I had power like that, I wouldn't know what to do and I would probably be afraid to use it. I was also amazed because He was controlling the whole situation. Can you believe that even during these times He was still using His power?

After watching the Ten Commandments, I went straight to the chapter of Exodus in the bible to read about God. In the past, many people kept on sinning and God was so merciful that He didn't destroy the whole planet. Can you believe it? God has the power to destroy the whole planet! We know that God created the earth since it's in the first chapter called Genesis from the bible. What fascinates me is the fact that he still exists, and you can tell. If you read about Noah in the chapter of Genesis, you will understand why God chose him and why God made the great flood. You will notice God's power when he flooded the whole earth. People are noticing that God allows floods to exist today. During the time of Noah, people kept sinning and God had to flood the whole earth. Have you noticed that he allowed the floods to exist, but he hasn't flooded the whole earth? Why? In the chapter with Noah, it mentions that God will make a covenant between you and Him as a reminder that He will NOT ever flood the whole earth again. The covenant sign is the rainbow in the sky. Haven't you noticed every time there's a rainbow in the sky, it pops up after a sun shower? It rains and then the sun comes out and you must look around you to find the rainbow. God is reminding us that He will keep His word that He will not ever flood the whole earth again. It's cool! Isn't it beautiful to know that God exists? Isn't it beautiful to realize that no matter what, God is still in control?

Some people feel it's strange to say He is our Father because He's God, not human. As for me, I put Him in the category as our Father because He created us, and He is love. I also put Him in a category where He loves like a human being. Have you ever sat and wondered what God is doing? How does He think about us? How much does He love us? I have no idea what God is doing now or when He uses His power or where He is always. As a Christian, I know that God is all-knowing. It's a learning process. When you're in a relationship, you are in a commitment. It's not easy because there are times when you do not feel like praying or reading but in a committed relationship you must make the time. You must work at it. I face this myself. It's not easy but the beauty with God is that His door is always open for you to come back to Him. Have conversations with Him. It's important to take the time to learn about Jesus. Jesus was an example of how we should live among each other in humanity.

I remember every year they would show on television the story of Jesus of Nazareth. It was another story in the Bible to read about because He represented how we should live among each other to save humanity. Many people I come across say things like, "the Bible is distorted the Bible is not true, and Jesus is not coming back." I would ask them, "How do you know? Did you read the Bible?" They say no. I would say, "Then how could you make that comment if you haven't read the bible?" You're just going by what people tell you but you're not reading the Scripture for yourself to find out. He gave us examples of how to deal with situations. During these times, they would stone people who committed a sin. They showed in the movie, Jesus of Nazareth that the adulterous woman was about to get stoned. One of the Pharisees asked Jesus what he thought they should do. Was it right to stone the woman? Stoning the woman would kill her and killing is considered a sin. The Pharisees then asked should they let her free. If she is freed, then it would be permission for women to get away with adultery. Jesus knew that they asked this question in front of everyone to see what answer was going to come out and he knew the Pharisees were still trying to prove that He was not the true Messiah. Jesus simply said, "He who has not sinned cast the first stone."

I was in such awe of his answer because he showed that no one is perfect. He showed that we are all sinners so we shouldn't judge. He made it clear that man has no right to say what she's doing was right or wrong. They're not God! He was showing how we should not criticize each other. He was showing how we should live peacefully among each other.

Jesus later asked the woman, "Where are your accusers?" "Are they here to condemn you?" The woman replied, "I don't see them."

Jesus simply said, "Well, since your accusers are gone then I will not condemn you. Go and sin no more."

Wasn't that amazing? The violence just stopped! It was beautiful to see how everything went back to peace. Jesus represented peace. As Christians, we are considered followers of Christ. We believe in the Father, the Son, and the Holy Spirit. Jesus is considered the son of God. We are followers of Christ so we should represent peace. Therefore, we cannot put limitations on God because Jesus was also showing us that we are not in a position like God to say what is right and what is wrong since we are not perfect. We are all sinners. When the violence stopped, it showed how powerful God is. If you incorporate Jesus into your life, you will get to know the power of God. You will understand how God wants you to live life His way so you can live in peace. He doesn't want bad things for you!

He is like a parent to a child. Your parents always want what's best for you. Jesus was known as the Prince of Peace! He wants what's best for you. 2. Do you know that Jesus taught us how to pray? Scripture tells us to close the door and pray in silence alone with God. It's a way to communicate with him and you can hear Him with no distractions. It's a way to hear Him clearly and He can hear you. Matthew Chapter 6, Verse 6 (KJV). It speaks.

But thou, when thou pray, enter thy closet, and when thou hast shut thy door

Pray to thy Father which is in secret; and thy Father which seeth in secret shall reward thee openly.

This is is an example of where to pray and how to do it. It's amazing!

It's good to pray everyday. There are a lot of people that I hear are too busy and they find it hard to find the time to pray.

It's not easy but you can do it if you incorporate it into your schedule. You should really find the time to pray because God should be in everything you do.

GOD should come first in everything. He is our creator. The scripture tells us how we should eat, how we should live, and how we should act.

God has the power to do so He can do anything because He can. Remember what God told Moses, "I AM that I AM." God can do all things. He has the power to do whatever He wants! Why am I telling you all this? I'm telling you all this because I'm demonstrating how I know certain things about God and how I built that relationship with God to be able to discern his voice.

God had to send a part of Himself to save us from the captivity of sin. I'm so glad we serve a merciful God! He is amazing!

3. There's another way how I discern the voice of God is to test the spirits.

From this Bible chapter, we can see how to discern the spirits to know whether they are coming from God or not. In Chapter 1, John 4:1-6 (KJV), it states:

Beloved, believe not every spirit, but try the spirits whether they are of God;

Because many false prophets are gone out into the world.

Hereby know ye the Spirit of God; Every spirit that confesses that Jesus Christ

Is come in the flesh is of God:

And every spirit that confesses not that Jesus Christ comes in the flesh is not of God;

And this is that of antichrist, whereof ye have heard that it should come, and even now

Already is it in the world.

Ye are of God, little children, and have overcome them: because greater is he that is in

You, then he that, is in the world.

They are of the world: therefore, speak they of the world, and the world heareth them.

We are of God; he that knoweth God heareth us; he that is not of God heareth not us.

Hereby know we the spirit of truth, and the spirit of error.

There are a lot of false prophets, but this is why we need to focus on God and not stray away from Him. We are going through some tough times, and we are definitely at the end of the days.

We must try to do the will of the Lord. I also notice how God communicated with people in the bible. I would see how He communicated with people like Abraham, Moses Noah, Job, and King David as examples. When I read stories about these people in the Bible, I get fascinated by how God chose them and used them in a mighty way. I realize God can speak to you, but you must distinguish the difference between your own thoughts and God's voice. 4. What I usually do sometimes is that I ask in prayer if it's really God or I just test it. For example, I went to Israel. I was on the plane and most people that were on the plane were Orthodox Jews. Before the plane took off, I was nervous because I remembered God told me to go to Israel. I was scared to find out what God wanted to tell me. I remember I heard in my head the voice said, "I am with you. Meet me in Israel." At that moment, this is when I tested to see if that was God. I prayed and asked God if you are with me then let someone come in front of me to pray and someone came in front of me and did. Sometimes, I would think it's probably a coincidence so I would ask again because I wanted to confirm if it was really God. It happened again and another man prayed in front of me. I was a little scared at first, but it made me realize that God was really talking to me. Sometimes, God will tell you things and you're not sure if it's Him and His confirmation would come after you hear the voice.

I was already shocked, and I realized God was serious. What does He sound like? I don't know how it would sound to most people, but He does sound like a human being. It will be loud in your head. Sometimes it may be a small voice. He would never sound like He was yelling most of the time and I would test it and say, "God is that you?" If it is, prove it or show me. He's not going to put you in an uncomfortable situation that would make you do things that do not fit His character. God is all-knowing. He even knows beforehand what you're going to say through prayer. You can't hide from Him because He's everywhere.

The beauty with God is that He gives us the freedom of choice. You can tell people are still sinning, but they can choose. There are a lot of people that don't care about how they should live according to His will. I guess people sin because it makes them feel good. It makes them feel like they don't have to follow the rules. Some people think it's a little boring following the rules, but the rules set things in order. It creates organization and peace. What people don't realize is that the more you create violence, chaos, and destruction, you're really destroying yourselves. Therefore, God decided to give us the freedom of choice. Are you on God's side or the Devil's side? We already know God will always win! There are times I ask myself why did God choose me? I always felt that I wasn't good enough to deserve to be chosen by the Great Almighty because I know I'm not perfect. I always wondered what it was about me that GOD chose me to communicate with. Sometimes, I would have a problem deciding and I would pray about it then I would find out about it the next day. I guess it's because I always look to Him and am fascinated by His power. When I hear his voice, I know God is not going to force me into something that is not for me. In other words, God is not going to give you something you cannot bear. If He feels you can't do the job, He will not give it to you if you can't handle it. You will know that God is with you every step of the way.

It takes time to discern his voice and it takes practice. You will know His voice soon enough when you realize it is different than your conscious. There are people who hear the voice of God all the time and never skip a beat. May God continue to bless them. 5. Sometimes, I would have a problem making a decision and I would, and I would pray about it and I would find out the next day. There are times you're not going to get an answer right away from God. God's timing is perfection, so you must wait and be patient. Most of the time things happen in His time.

Most of the time when God speaks to you, He will do it in a way to grab your attention. He will repeat it to you repeatedly. You may think it's your conscious, but this is when you read Scripture and test the spirits.

In the Chapter of 1 John 4;2-3, it says any spirit that confesses that Jesus Christ comes in the flesh is of God and any spirit that does not confess that Jesus Christ comes in the flesh is of the antichrist. It's not going to be easy, but it takes practice, and usually, God will tell you things that are for your own good. It is according to His will. He wants what's best for you because God is love. 6. There may be times when God may tell you to do something, and you may not feel comfortable with it or like it. You must test it.

In the Bible, God had asked Abraham to sacrifice his son. In the Book of Genesis Chapter 22;1-2 it says:

And it came to pass after these things that God did tempt Abraham, and said unto him,

Abraham: and he said, Behold, here I am.

And he said, Take now thy son, thine only son Isaac, whom thou lovest, and get thee

Into the land of Moriah, and offer him there for a burnt offering upon one of the

Mountains which I will tell thee of.

The whole point of repeating this story is that you must be prepared if God tells you things or asks you to do things that may not make any sense to you. He's God! How can we understand him? His mind is infinitely great and so we cannot comprehend or imagine the way God works. You can read the rest of the chapter, but it seemed crazy. Would you sacrifice one of your own kids as an offering? Why would God ask him to do that? If you keep reading the chapter, you will realize that Abraham was going to do what God told him to do and the Angel said, it's ok, here I am. You don't have to take your knife and use him for sacrifice. Well, it wasn't exactly how I said it, but when you read Chapter 22 in the book of Genesis you will realize it was a test. Yep! I said it! It was a test! Sometimes, God may ask you to do something, and it will be a test. You just must hear God's voice, obey and you will find out later its purpose.

7. You'd be surprised how sometimes God may ask you something and you're wondering if it's Him and your answer may come from another person. God can use people to guide you to what he wants you to do. I remember God told me that I was going to leave my home where I was living in the Northeast. He told me that I would have to leave. I didn't have a lot of money and I didn't have a place to go. I had no idea how I was going to leave. God used one of my close friends, Esther, to suggest for me to attend college. I didn't

think about going to college was my way out and it was putting me through training for what God wanted me to do.   I didn't realize it right away, but as certain things came to pass by what was told to me by Ms. Queen, I realized it was really God.   I just didn't realize how it was going to prepare me for the adventure I was about to take.   My experience hearing God's voice was amazing.   I had no idea where my life was going.

I usually am in control and know which way to go or what to do but now I just live my life following God's voice.   I'm no longer in control.   God controls my life now!   The things that I really wanted to do God didn't lead me in that direction because it was not going to glorify His name.   God had to be in the center of everything and I'm glad I left home because I wouldn't have experienced the beauty of what God had done around the world.   God would tell me things and I would always ask God, "How is that going to happen?" "When will it take place?" Or "Who am I to do this?" "God, am I really good at what you want me to do?" "Can I handle it?" "Am I good enough?" God will show you and lead you to your journey.   Everyone's journey is different.   It's not going to be an easy road either.   My experience in doing the Lord's will in certain places sometimes was a battle.   There were many days that I cried and wished it ended but God was with me every step of the way.

God's People! It's time to hold the armor of God!

I have shared with you my journey with God. I'm a normal human being like everyone else. I have no idea why I was chosen but I'm not the only one chosen in this world. God has a way to pick people to do His will so people can be saved. I've met so many people in my life that God had used to help me and to guide me to my journey with Him. I've learned that life is not going to be easy, but you just got to get back up and stand up for the Lord!

We live in a world where we want things now and right away. If we did things our way most of the time sometimes it can lead to destruction. When you wait on the Lord, it will be God's timing. Check this verse out!

In Psalms 27:14 (KJV), it says:

Wait on the Lord; be of good courage, and he shall strengthen thine heart: wait, I say, on the Lord.

The psalms were written by Kind David and God loved him so much! King David loved the Lord, and you will see his story in Chapters 1 Samuel and 2, Samuel.

If you look around, you know things are getting a little crazy. The evils of this world are taking over. The people of evil have their job to do and we as saints have our job to do. Any demonic activity that is taking place in the world will not last long since their time will be up. This world is not forever!

We have no time to half-step nowadays. Look around you and you'll see in the news what's happening with the earthquakes, the hurricanes, the bombings and people crashing into mosques, the school shootings, police brutality, etc.....

Don't worry about why bad things are happening or why God lets this happen to us. We suffered for so long but remember we are no longer in captivity of sin. God knew we were going to keep sinning, so we got saved when Jesus died on the cross for us. This whole battle is the Great Controversy between Good and Evil. We already know that God is going to win. God always wins so stay alert and keep on the Word. The Book of Revelations, it's already telling us and showing us what will be taking place. Those who believe in Jesus are on God's side. I don't know about you, but I would rather get on the winner's side. Those who don't know who Jesus is, just take the time to get to know him!

Take courage and stand up for the Lord, no matter what happens. God sees all these things. God is watching and He's in control. We're going to go through some tough times, but God's people get ready! This is the time, God's people that we need to stay focused on Jesus. Why? The reason why is because the world knows that the second coming of Christ is supposed to take place. You must know who the anti-Christ is and who the real Jesus is. How will you know if you don't keep on the Bible? The Old Testament exists from the Bible. The New Testament is the story of Jesus. Jesus is the way, the truth, and the life! It worked for me! Those who have witnessed the miraculous experience with Jesus ask them and they will tell you!

Most people make it through when they make God a part of their lives. You cannot win against God if you're against him. Stay alert by reading the Scripture and acknowledging the signs around you. You should try to build a relationship with Him so you will have an overflow of blessings and peace.

Don't be afraid to talk to God. God is everywhere and He will listen to you.

There may be some people who are struggling to reach out to the Lord. There are those that are trapped in bondage. Don't give up! God knows if you just turn to Him. He knows when you were crying, and He knows the heartache and He knows the pain and the struggle you're facing. He knows all things. Through the midst of all that is happening today just focus on Jesus. If you are a non-believer of Jesus, take the time to get to know his ways. Read about him! If you don't like to read, then rent videos about him. It will not hurt you if you just give it a shot! Do not let the enemy wear you out! The enemy will try to trick you. Your enemy maybe someone close to you. Let's prepare by reading Scripture with faith, hope, and love. It's a crazy world out there but we can overcome any obstacle by learning about Jesus! In the Chapter of John 16:33 (KJV), it says:

These things I have spoken unto you, that in me ye might have peace. In the world ye shall have tribulation: but be of good cheer; I have overcome the world.

I have spoken peace to you but in the world, you should have tribulation.

Well, as Christians, we are not going to go through life easily either. We're going to go through some suffering. When Jesus walked the earth and did his mission, he went through some trials himself. We know that God was within him, and Jesus had the chance to experience what it was like to live among us. Jesus suffered so what makes you think we're not going to go through the suffering also? God's people suffered for a long time but now it's time to take courage.

All we must do is turn to God and repent. Have a conversation with Him and say, "God, I messed up and I'm sorry. Please forgive me." If it's really a struggle and it's difficult then tell God to help you take the desires of whatever the sin is away. I know people who do immoral things know the difference between what is good and what is bad. It's better to be in peace than to deal with drama all the time. Some people feed off drama and they like chaos. If you surround yourself with drama all the time, chances are you're going to go through drama yourself.

I probably would not have had the opportunity to travel the world and be at peace if I didn't follow God's ways. I would probably have chaos in my life all the time. I wanted so badly to be part of the world of entertainment, but I realized that God had a better plan, and it really took me a long time to accept it. I'm now at a point in my life where I'm so glad that I accepted following Christ all the way. I couldn't see it at the time because I wanted that type of lifestyle like the rich and famous but now, I'm happy in Jesus that I don't regret it at all. I'm with people who are in the business, but I hear so many stories as to how they had to suffer sometimes. I would hear that there were times that they wished they had some peace and serenity. It's not easy in the entertainment world but it does feel like being part of the club. God let me know that he had a better plan for me, and he wanted me to join His club. Sometimes, I think people in the entertainment business were chosen because they can handle it.

For those who are in the business and struggling, just hang in there and turn to Jesus. Schedule some time to pray and repent… They draw such an enormous fan base that if they just continue to set an example, it would be tough for them to act like Jesus when they're surrounded by temptation all the time. It's important for them to remove themselves sometimes and take a break. Your health is much more important. You must prepare for that type of life, mentally and spiritually. It's important for people in that business to find time to break and talk to God for guidance. He knows what you're going through so you just must find time to pray in your busy schedule. I like to hear celebrities like Justin Bieber, Kevin Hart, Nick Cannon, Jim Cavaziel, Denzel Washington, Chris Pratt to name a few who are not afraid to talk about Jesus. In the United States, there is freedom of religion so it's beautiful to hear them express their beliefs. It's ok! We need to understand and learn from each other. I recently saw a video and saw the artists from Puerto Rico, and I realized Marc Anthony made the sign of the cross. It was beautiful to see that! It's hard to act like Jesus in that world of entertainment because of the distractions and the chaos but they can survive if they just take the time out in their busy schedule and turn to him.

In order to see what's in the darkness, we must put on the light. The two together have their own jobs. The people who are in darkness do things in the dark. The people who are in the light will do the things that are in the light. You need to know your enemy. I've learned from my experience that not everyone is your friend. Can you imagine that the one closest to you can sometimes be your enemy? It could even be a family member. How will you know? Test the spirits and their character. Do they act according to God's will? I know we're not perfect and that's the beauty about Jesus. He knows that we're going to sin so because he saved us from being in captivity of sin. All we must do is turn to Him and repent. Isn't that wonderful?

You have a choice to choose whose side you want to be on. Do you want to get into the light or get into the darkness? Well, let me make it easier for you to choose. How about thinking about the consequences after you die? God already made it clear that this is not our home because we are all waiting for the second coming of our Lord and Savior, Jesus Christ. God is preparing a new home for us. I sometimes think about people who've died and had so many materialistic things, but these things did not go with them when they die. It's important not to serve two masters. You cannot serve money and God at the same time. It's ok to have a lot of money but it's what you do with it that is important.

Have you ever wondered that you would live to see these last days? We are in the last days because of the signs that were told to us in the book of Revelation.

In 1 John 2:22 (KJV), it says:

Who is a liar but he that denieth that Jesus is the Christ? He is the antichrist, that denieth the Father and the Son.

In 1 John 4:3 (KJV)< it says:

And every spirit confesseth not that Jesus Christ comes in the flesh is not of God: and this is that spirit of antichrist, whereof ye have heard that it should come, and even now already is it in the world.

In 2 John 1:7 (KJV), it says:

For many deceivers are entered into the world, who confess not that Jesus Christ comes in the flesh. This is a deceiver and an antichrist.

I can't imagine how anyone would want to go against God! God's people, it's time to stand up for the Lord! Know who you represent! You are a child of God! You are the child of the Highest! God is the creator of all nations! He is the King of Kings and Lord of Lords! He is our way maker! He is our provider! He is our God in battle! He is the Alpha, the Omega, and the beginning and the end! He is the Great I AM! He is the King of the universe and the architect of the universe! He is omnipresent! He is omniscient! He is omnipotent! He is the first and the last! He is undefeated! Armies can't defeat him! Leaders can't ignore him! He is Holy! He is eternal! He is our savior! He is our comfort! He is the ruler of rulers! He will not ever forsake you and forget you! He will not overlook you! He will make the time represent, God's people! Stand up and know we serve a mighty God! Stand up and know that God is for us and so who can be against us! Right now, you better give Him praise! When you face any battle, any tribulation, remember! God is with you every step of the way! When you face your enemy in battle just remember who you represent! NO ONE! NO ONE! NO ONE! IS ABOVE GOD!

God's people! This book was written to show that God exists today. This is the testimony of my life with the Lord. I never thought that God was going to choose me to see the beauty of what He has done in my life. I have to thank the Lord for saving me and guiding me. God is my provider, my savior, my father, my everything! I wouldn't know what to do if God wasn't in my life. God wants what's best for you too. We will be going home soon! Jesus will come like a thief in the night. We don't know if it will be tomorrow, next week or next year. We cannot comprehend God's thinking, but He loves us so much that He wants us to go home with Him and live in peace forever. Much love for God's people! Let's continue to spread God's love all over the world and continue to do His will so we can enter the kingdom of heaven. Amen!